THE
BUSINESS OF
MEDICINE

The Definitive Guide to Help New Physicians
Start Their Career on the Right Path
and Avoid Costly Mistakes

TUNG GIEP M.D.

To my wife, Michelle.
You have been the light in my hour of need.

Visit TheBusinessofMedicine.net
for resources

CONTENTS

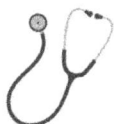

PREFACE

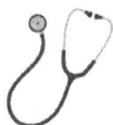

I was born in South Vietnam during the Vietnam War. My dad was an OB/GYN. He completed his training in Vietnam and his residency in the US at the Women's College of Pennsylvania. My mother was a housewife who raised four boys, all of us eventually becoming physicians. We fled South Vietnam at the end of the war in 1975. Even today, I hold terrible memories of our evacuation from Vietnam. The chaotic scene of the US withdrawal from Afghanistan in 2021 elicited my post-traumatic stress disorder and reminded me of my departure from Vietnam. I was just fourteen years old when all this happened, so I remember things quite vividly.

Throughout most of my pre-teen years, I recall my dad having some quite colorful physician friends, many of whom seemed to be

Future doctor with my mother.
1960s in Saigon Vietnam

very important Americans. They were part of the physician teaching exchange program from America. One night, my dad came home and insisted we have a family meeting. His American friends had told him that something big would be happening soon. The Americans were abandoning South Vietnam.

"We need to listen to the Voice of America radio show over the next few days," my dad told us. "Listen continuously. When you hear a Christmas song played in dedication, that's the signal that the Americans are bugging out. They are evacuating all US dependents."

A Christmas song in April? I thought. We waited and waited, listening to the radio all day that first day. Same thing on day two. Finally, it happened after two days of waiting and listening. I believe the song was "White Christmas." As soon as we heard it, the entire family flew into action. The plan was to get our family out of the country using my brother's American passport and claiming that

With my family in Saigon Vietnam. New Year's Day 1972.

we were all US dependents. My brother, who was only nine years old in 1975, was born in the US while my dad was in residency in Pennsylvania. We were able to get into the airport with one of my dad's American friends, but without my dad; he entered differently. My dad, being of military age, had to be smuggled into the airport by taxi so he wouldn't be grabbed and forced to fight in the South Vietnam military. Dad and his friend had forged some documents claiming that my mom was married to my dad's friend, and that we were part of his family. Thankfully, that all worked, and my dad made it inside the airport safely and joined the rest of our family.

Once the entire family was inside the Tan Son Nhat airport, we proceeded to the US consulate located in a makeshift office onsite. My dad proceeded to use my brother's passport to claim he was a US dependent. Unfortunately, he was denied the opportunity to evacuate with the rest of us. Despite his disappointment with the decision, he listened to my mother who advised him to try again the next day. That evening, the crowds of refugees grew larger and larger. Word had spread that the Americans were leaving, and everyone wanted out. We spent the night on the tennis court next to the US consulate grounds. That night, the president of Vietnam, Nguyen Van Thieu, resigned and fled the country on a Boeing plane from the same airport. That's when things really began to fall apart.

In the morning, the US consulate still wouldn't allow anyone to leave who wasn't a US dependent. By noon, US marines had arrived in helicopters to start evacuation procedures. Heavily armed marines formed a perimeter around the consulate and assisted in burning all papers and equipment inside the compound with huge bonfires. There was a sense of urgency with a lot of pushing, shoving, and screaming followed by occasional bursts of gunfire to keep the crowd at bay. The US consulate finally appeared and announced that everyone inside the compound would be evacuated with the President. He then left in a helicopter for a naval ship anchored offshore. After waiting in limbo for two days, we finally got permission to leave.

As several C-130 transport planes descended slowly and landed in a line atop the tarmac, droves of desperate people clamored to board. When our turn came, thoughts of my life as I knew it flashed through my mind. I was just a kid, awkward, witty, and smart. Like other fourteen-year-olds, I wondered what would become of our neighbors, my school friends, the rest of our family. I thought of our home and my belongings, which all had to be left behind. None of that mattered now. All of that was coming to an end. I had no idea what the future had in store for me, for us. *Will I land in the USA tomorrow? Will we be able to remain together as a family? Where will we live?*

Suddenly, gunfire erupted and I heard a loud boom. The Viet Cong was now shelling the airport. Small arms fire could be heard coming from the edge of the runway and people scrambled for safety. All of the commotion only served to heighten the urgency to get on board. Even the young American marines were now nervous and swiftly ushered us onto the enormous grey plane that looked like a giant whale with wings and propellers. Once on board, there were no chairs or seats; only a long, thick rope pulled tightly across the inside deck of the plane.

Two airmen were stationed inside the bay of the plane, one on each side. At take off, one of the airmen fired flares out the window. The other had a machine gun and fired down toward the ground; at what, I did not know. I didn't want to know. Not a word was spoken by anyone inside the plane. Hearing only muffled whimpers from children and women, I held my breath for what seemed like an hour until the pilot made an announcement that we had left Vietnam's airspace. A loud applause and cheers rang out. We were now officially on our way to the United States.

Our first stop was Clark Air Force Base in the Philippines. With free-flowing soft drinks and potato chips offered to us, I thought I must be in heaven. After about a week there, we again boarded a plane, this time bound for Guam, a small island in the middle of the

Pacific Ocean. Upon arrival, all I could see was a sea of blue tents, presumably our housing during our time there. As it turned out, that *was* our housing, but those tents were empty. Conditions were miserable. There were no beds to sleep on, so we slept on bare dirt until we were able to get a hold of some cardboard to serve as a thin layer between the dusty ground and our tired bodies. Latrines were limited, so the beach became our bathroom. The mess hall was about a half-mile walk from the tented areas where we slept, and the food was terrible; typical cafeteria food, but it was better than nothing. We stayed in Guam for about seven months and then transferred to Camp Pendleton, just north of San Diego in California. We had gone from the hot, tropical climate of Vietnam to the cold, dry climate of Southern California. Yes, it was cold there, especially when you're used to ninety-degree humidity on a daily basis.

During this time, my dad volunteered as an interpreter at the camp's infirmary. This gave him some insight into how things were run on base and an opportunity to meet individuals who might help us relocate to a more stable living environment. With him gone during the day, I watched over the family, making sure we kept a close eye on the few belongings in our possession. We had nothing except a few clothes and my dad's diplomas proving he had graduated from a university in the US. That seemed to be our ticket to success, so we held his diplomas very close. We stayed there almost eight months until my dad found a sponsor for our family. It turned out to be one of my dad's former acquaintances from the physician teaching exchange program he had participated in earlier when he was in Vietnam.

From Southern California, we moved to Augusta, Georgia. What a culture shock! I already knew English before we came to Augusta, so the language was not a barrier to me. However, I was placed into ninth grade immediately upon my arrival. In Vietnam, we were already learning calculus. While in Augusta, it was algebra 1. The kids in my class decided to give me a nickname: Bruce. At the time, I didn't understand why they chose that as my nickname. Years later, I learned that my classmates thought my brothers and I all knew kung fu. Hollywood star Bruce Lee was quite popular then, and served as their reference point for Americans previously unfamiliar with Asians; therefore, I was Bruce to them.

We stayed in Augusta for a year before my dad took a job with a private OB/GYN practice in Spartanburg, South Carolina, where we were one of the few Asian families living in the community. During that year, our family did our best to acclimate to the culture. Needless to say, it was difficult. One evening, our family walked into a local seafood restaurant for dinner. As we entered the establishment and stood at the reception area waiting to be seated, the entire room full of patrons and servers froze and stared at us. It was one of the most uncomfortable experiences I'd had in my young life. But after a while, they all got used to us.

Over the years, my family stayed in Spartanburg, South Carolina, and I remained there for my undergraduate studies at Wofford College. By the time I graduated, I was twenty-two years old and felt like I was firmly a part of American culture, although I never forgot my home in Vietnam. As graduation approached, so did the time to apply to medical school. While my classmates applied to ten to fifteen schools, I applied to only three. As a result, my dad thought I wasn't serious about getting into medical school. He asked what my plan B was. I told him the three medical schools are the ones where I had the best chance of getting accepted.

"If I don't get in, I'll go into international business or culinary school," I said.

Why culinary school you might ask? Well, being the oldest of four boys, my parents would host dinner parties at our house. Since there wasn't a girl in our family, I had the dubious honor of being the sous chef. I got really good at cooking, especially, Asian cuisine. Thankfully—and much to my parents' relief—I was accepted to two out of the three medical schools I applied to. The rest is history.

Throughout my medical career, I have made mistakes and I've made some smart moves. Best of all, I've learned the business of medicine. I am proud to share what I've learned in hopes that you can avoid some of my mistakes, make a way for yourself, and build a career—and possibly a business—that you are proud of. In the process, my hope is that you are fortunate enough to work with a group of talented physicians and an organization you are proud to be part of, as I am today.

INTRODUCTION

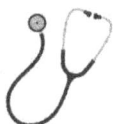

You are about to complete—or perhaps you have just finished—your residency, fellowship, physician assistant, or nurse practitioner training. You're at the end of a years-long journey that has brought you from a fledgling student with nothing but a desire to help people, through one of the most arduous courses of study known to mankind, to a place of satisfaction, relief, and . . . well, confusion.

What now? That is the question every new medical school graduate has, and it's a necessary question to ask and answer for yourself.

You are starting a new chapter in your life that you are quite ill-prepared for. That's the truth. Take it from me because I've been there. After being in private practice for seventeen years, I grew my practice and operated one of the largest multi-specialty private practices in Texas with over 150 employees and physicians covering four cities and fifteen hospitals. Eventually, I sold the practice to a publicly traded company on the New York Stock Exchange in 2017. By most standards, my story would be considered a success. From where I stand, growing my career to that level was one of the hardest, emotionally draining things I have ever done.

Over those twenty plus years, I sacrificed my time, marriage, and family relationships. Was it worth it? Well, that answer isn't easy. The important thing is that I learned a lot. This book is written to help you avoid some of the pitfalls I encountered and to understand some of the lessons I learned.

This new chapter in your life is one that all those years of clinical training didn't prepare you for. Sure, you've studied *Gray's Anatomy*, *Harrison's Principles of Internal Medicine*, *Smith's Recognizable Pattern of Human Malformation*, *Williams Obstetrics*, and more. You have learned to do procedures, document electronic medical records, diagnose disease processes, deal with different family dynamics, and handle death. But none of that fully prepared you for what's next: your first job in the medical field and the business of medicine.

> ***Sadly, your studies haven't prepared you for the real world of being a doctor.***

A world of excitement awaits you as you begin your career in the real world. As a medical professional, you will join an elite group of experts who are respected and admired by society. How you approach this prestigious position, and all the opportunities that come with it, will have a profound impact on your opinion of whether all the sacrifices you've endured up to this point were worth it. The world needs medical professionals. Sadly, your studies haven't prepared you for the real world of being a doctor. You've learned the clinical side of medicine, but you haven't been exposed to the business side of medicine . . . until now. I will enlighten you on this side of medicine and help you understand what goes on inside boardrooms and how decisions are made, decisions that affect you and your career.

Medicine is a business, plain and simple. Sure, the world sees the medical industry as the life-saving force that heals and cures. That is the outside view. From the inside, it's a whole different story.

My journey in neonatology began at 7:00 a.m. sharp at Children's Mercy Hospital in Kansas City. The possibility to earn a start to my fellowship had me questioning my choice of specialization and my confidence as a physician. Standing there in the office of Dr. R. T. Hall—the "Father of Neonatology in the Midwest"—I was as nervous as I've ever been. This man wrote the book on neonatal nutrition and had the reputation for expecting certainty and accuracy from his fellows.

"Son, you must be here for an interview," he said as I entered his office.

"Yes, sir," I replied, as if I was responding to a drill sergeant.

After a few casual words, he led me to the neonatal ICU. This huge 50-bed, Level-4 intensive care unit was more than intimidating for me. There, I saw teams of doctors with different specialties rounding on their patients. Surgical service, infectious disease, cardiology, and gastroenterology all did their morning routine like a choreographed dance around the many incubators and ventilators. I could have sworn those incubators would part like the Red Sea as the attendings walked by. Then, it was our turn to do our neonatal rounds.

As we approached the first patient and the intern completed his presentation of overnight events, Dr. Hall asked me, "What would you do for this patient?"

I offered my reply, to which he nodded in approval. I exhaled in relief. He then told the intern, "Do it." We did the same with a second patient. Again, my treatment suggestion was appropriate. *Great. I'm on a roll here*, I thought to myself, being cautious not to get too full of myself.

When we came to the third patient, the attending asked what I thought of the skin rash on the baby. *Yikes! Dermatology was my weakest subject in school.* I stalled by asking more clinical questions. I'm pretty sure he could tell I was buying time. Finally, I decided.

"Based on everything I know about the patient's clinicals and how the rash presents, I'd say zinc deficiency."

As soon as I said it, I had a sinking feeling in my gut. This was reenforced when Dr. Hall looked at me over the rim of his bifocals, smiling, and said, "That ain't zinc deficiency." After that, he didn't speak to me again for the rest of the rounds.

Slowly, I moved from the front of the team to the back of the crowd. A few hours later, the dermatology attending came over to Dr. Hall and tapped him on the shoulder. "That baby you consulted us on, we think he has zinc deficiency."

Dr. Hall immediately searched the crowd looking for me. When he located me in the back of the group, his eyes beamed with enthusiasm as he said, "Son, I don't know how you got that, but we need you. Go down to my office and sign some papers. The interview is over."

Wow, what a relief!

After completing my three years of fellowship training in neonatology, I was ready to face the real world and practice what I had learned. I was reminded of the many lessons I had learned during my time at Children's Mercy Hospital. My first patient with diaphragmatic hernia was extremely sick. After coming off extracorporeal membrane oxygenation (heart/lung bypass), my patient was on seven different medical drips and on maximum ventilatory support to keep him alive. But he was doing poorly and I had to call the parents to request a withdrawal of life-sustaining support.

When the mother arrived, she went to the child's bedside and combed his hair back then whispered something into his ear. Immediately, his oxygen saturation improved. With excitement, the mother called me over to say, "I think he likes hearing my voice." She then asked me why I had called this meeting. I couldn't bring myself to tell her that I wanted to withdraw support. So, I told her I wanted her to stay by the bedside and sing to her baby. She did. Wouldn't you know that baby never looked back. He was discharged home about six months later. Despite all the knowledge and science we had to offer as physicians, it was still the touch and sound of a loving mother that turned things around. That lesson was never lost on me. I was ready to leave the nest and strike out on my own with all this knowledge and wisdom.

I learned about my first job in much the same fashion you are aware of. While attending a medical conference in Kansas City, I was approached by a recruiter and we quickly became friends. She told me about this wonderful up-and-coming national group. Many prestigious people had joined this group, which had plans to go public with an IPO. It all sounded great—the promises of a quick hire, a fat salary, advancement opportunities at a national practice, and to have ownership through stock options. Little did I know that these recruiters get paid by commission, typically a percentage of your first-year salary. So, there's an incentive to get you to sign. Remember, it's business, not personal.

With a mix of excitement and uncertainty bubbling inside of me, I threw caution to the wind, accepted the offer, and signed the contract without much thought. I read through the legalese and was told that everything was standard in the industry. After all, I trusted my newfound friends at the recruitment agency. They had done this a thousand times for a thousand successful doctors, I told myself. I packed my bags and moved to Southern Florida, ready to impart all those lessons I had learned in Kansas City.

Sadly, like you, I didn't know how the business of medicine worked. I trusted those recruiters, thinking they had my best interest at heart. They didn't. I was naive. I didn't understand my contract before signing it and, therefore, didn't notice the clause stipulating the requirement that I was responsible to purchase tail malpractice insurance should I leave the practice. This was to protect me from any future lawsuit from the time I was employed by the group.

When I arrived at my new job, I was overjoyed. The staff and other doctors were nice and civil. The patients were cordial and compliant with my diagnoses and instructions. Life was good . . . until it wasn't.

After seven months into the job, I received a letter of complaint from a former patient's parents about my bill. I foolishly told them that it must be a mistake and that I would investigate it. With a quick call to the billing department asking them to investigate the error, I went along with business as usual, treating patients and managing my workload, including communicating with the family that had sent the letter. A couple of days later, I received a certified letter from my company's corporate attorney. It was a cease-and-desist order stating that any further contact with the family would result in my immediate termination from the practice and possible legal actions against me. Imagine the fear I had about my first job ending in such a legal disaster.

In the days following that heartbreaking letter, I didn't know what to think or do. So, I scheduled a meeting with my medical director. He told me that he had intended to talk to me anyway about my lack of productivity. According to him, I hadn't been aggressive enough in admitting patients for procedures or tests that would keep them in the hospital for several days, thereby increasing billing opportunities for the practice. I was confused about this. Until that point, I had remained committed to the tried-and-true philosophy in neonatology: "Baby sick, you admit." If the patient didn't need to be admitted, and could be observed in the mother's room, that was best for the child and the family. Apparently, that wasn't the way things worked under his guidance. He then made some suggestions on how I could increase my admission rate. This was contrary to what I had learned during my years of training. I decided that this kind of drama and stress was not for me. I resigned. This was not the experience of medicine I had envisioned. Years later, I understood what my medical director was doing. He was climbing the corporate ladder. He was an MD with an MBA who later became a VP for the group. This was over twenty years ago. Things are a lot tighter now with many new regulations.

During my exit interview, I explained to the founder and CEO—another MD with an MBA—my reason for leaving. I mentioned the patient letter of complaint about billing, the attorney's certified letter, and what my medical director had suggested to me, without explaining anything further or admitting any wrongdoing. In the most nonchalant tone, he said, "It's just business. It's nothing personal. Just get with the program and be a team player," he said.

Hoping to hide my shock at this statement, I told him, "My mind is made up. I'm leaving."

Surprisingly, he didn't try to convince me to stay. When he told me that I had to purchase a tail malpractice insurance policy for my protection, I was speechless. Tail malpractice insurance? I had never heard of this. The insurance would cover me and the practice if the patient pursued any medical negligence claim. Apparently, tail insurance wasn't included in my original employment contract that I had signed, nor had I inquired about it during the negotiations. I didn't know to ask. I didn't understand what he was trying to convey until many years later. By purchasing the tail insurance myself, the company didn't have to spend that money on me. The cost was over $20,000, and I had to decide before I left the room whether to pursue it. He made me so paranoid that I felt I had to purchase it or else I would certainly be a target for a malpractice lawsuit. In retrospect, I didn't need to do this, but I didn't know then what I know today. Back then, that was a lot of money for someone just nine months out of fellowship training.

That was a hard and humiliating experience. I don't want you to have the same experience or make the same mistake. I want you to understand your contract, what is standard and what is not, and what you can and should negotiate. If you take nothing else from this book let it be this: The business of medicine involves profit and losses, power and control. Never forget that.

As you enter the real world of the business of medicine, I want you to be able to walk into your first job with your eyes wide open, knowing what you're getting yourself into, knowing everything you need to know to protect yourself, to advance at your place of employment, to succeed as a physician, and to understand the behind-the-scenes-movements of business and the politics that surround it.

This book will only work if you are willing to learn and change your approach and open your eyes to the forces at play behind the scenes. My objective here is to prepare new graduates like you to enter your career with eyes wide open, but also provide you with the information and insight to be a savvy medical professional who succeeds in the business of medicine. Knowledge is power. You may be thinking: How do I survive this environment? The simple answer is that there are a lot of physicians who thrive in this environment. If you know the regulations, how the system works, and who the players are, you should be able to maneuver within your own space and survive.

This book is for you if:

- you are about to finish your training in residency or fellowship programs, or you just graduated and are unhappy with your current situation;
- you are about to graduate from physician assistant or nurse practitioner school;
- you want to understand the employment contracts and how to negotiate as you enter a contract agreement;
- you want to eventually join a practice or start your own medical business;
- you want your medical career to live up to your highest dreams and expectations;
- you eventually want to retire from medicine with a sense of accomplishment and satisfaction; or
- you want to better understand the business of medicine.

> *The world of medicine is a business,*
> *plain and simple.*

Do you need an MBA to do your job as a physician?

This book is written to guide you in making the best decisions for yourself and to be aware of the pitfalls along the journey of being a physician. No matter what you were told in medical school, the world of medicine is a business, plain and simple. The sooner you realize that, the more likely you are to accomplish your goals and succeed in your career. This book will not make you a better business person. Unfortunately, not everyone is meant to be an entrepreneur or a business owner. Most physicians are horrible in business. We're good clinicians, but we were not taught to manage finances, which is a critical aspect of operating a successful business.

You've made it this far, so obviously you are highly intelligent and motivated toward success. Like those in other professions—whether an entrepreneur, office manager, certified financial analyst, or rocket scientist—you have adopted the traits of successful individuals. For example, you probably:

- set goals for yourself;
- are persistent and willing to adjust course to overcome obstacles;
- remain focused on getting great at what you do;
- are disciplined;
- take risks, invest in yourself, and believe in yourself; and
- engage in smart financial practices.

All of these attributes will serve you well as you begin your medical career. With these traits, you will certainly progress from an entry-level physician to a well-respected care provider and colleague. However, these characteristics won't be enough to help you navigate the business of medicine. Remember, you have just completed an intense medical school program and undergone residency or fellowship training, not business school. Sure, you can get an MBA and then you can read financials, manage time and people, excel at customer/patient service, understand complex legal contracts, and understand profit/loss statements. You might wonder what any of this has to do with being a doctor. At the onset, it all might seem irrelevant. After all, you got into this gig to help people, to save some lives, to make the world a better place. (Excuse me while I strum a few notes on my violin.) All of that is well and good. And yes, the world needs more physicians, for sure. But more than that, it needs smart people who practice medicine and provide care from the place of knowledge and abundance.

This book will help you become more understanding of the business you are in. You should get an MBA if you plan to climb the corporate ladder. But when you are just starting your career, it's best to learn your craft and get your feet wet. Being a certified physician executive (CPE) is another way to become a leader in medicine. This is a different path than an MBA. The CPE serves as liaison between the physician and management, supervises physicians, and participates in strategic meetings. An MBA helps you better understand the complex healthcare landscape. I wouldn't recommend getting an MBA or CPE until you have at least five years of experience under your belt as a practitioner.

This book is not a "get rich quick scheme," nor will it explain the role of all the players in this industry. It will not tell you how to set up a private practice. That's for the next book. It will also not set up false hopes for you if you seek to "live large and in charge" as some big wig with a fancy degree who knows it all and wants everyone to bow down to you. If you got into medicine for that reason you're already on the wrong track and headed for disaster.

What this book will do is to give you a basic understanding of your options for practicing medicine and what to expect with your first job as a physician. It will also give you some insights into the business side of medicine. It is definitely not an MBA course or a course for CPE.

Here, you will learn:

- your options for employment as a physician;
- what to look for in a medical practice;
- what to expect from your first or next employer so you don't get the short end of the stick;
- what questions to ask in the interview;
- how to prepare for your interview;
- what your employer wants from you (and what they don't), so you can move your career in the direction of *your* goals, not someone else's;
- what you need to pay attention to in any employment contract;
- how to get out of an employment contract;
- how to behave as a new physician associate; and
- how to handle the temptations of the physician's lifestyle.

As you read this book, you will learn some of the hidden truths about the business of medicine so you can become savvy about the career and lifestyle you are embarking on and avoid being taken advantage of.

If you're not quite sure you need to know all this business-y stuff in order to enjoy a successful career in the medical field, well . . . read on.

THE LANDSCAPE:
IT'S COMPLICATED

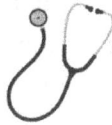

Medicine is a big business in the US, and you are now part of the healthcare industrial complex. Yes, you signed up for this business even before you knew what you were getting yourself into. But don't change your mind now. Instead of ripping up your medical diploma into a thousand pieces or setting it aflame on a sandy beach while you cry salty tears of regret, consider this your chance to learn how to make the most of your chosen career and emerge wiser, wealthier, and more well-grounded than you would be otherwise.

> *Like every other highly profitable industrial complex . . .*
> *the bottom line in the business of medicine is profit.*

As you begin your first real job in the medical field, you will soon be confronted with the reality that the *field* of medicine is actually the *business* of medicine. Like every other highly profitable industrial complex in our capitalist society—military, academic, prison, technology—the bottom line in the business of medicine is profit. There are several players in this intricate, heavily regulated system, including federal and state organizations, pharmaceutical corporations, insurance companies, private practices, nonprofit organizations, former and current federal/state legislators, lobbyists, and individual providers. The internal players include hospital administration, nursing staff, respiratory and physical therapists, social workers, home health providers, risk management, and system administrators. Then, there is the support system that includes medical consultants, in-house and outside legal counsel, medical malpractice attorneys, CPAs, financial advisors, and compliance officers. That's just the tip of the iceberg. Frankly, it's enough to make any physician want to give up after practicing for a few years. In fact, many do.

According to the American Medical Association (AMA), 1 in 5 doctors plans to leave medicine in the next two years.[1] You might become one of them. But don't jump ship too quickly. So, what causes physicians to be so dissatisfied that they change careers or even retire early? The biggest reason is due to burnout, some due to disillusionment with the system. Others are fed up with the challenges of running a business and losing money, while others quit because they've lost interest in medicine all together.

The business of medicine takes many years to learn and understand. After almost thirty years in the business—having practiced in corporate medicine, as an employed physician, in private practice, as a business owner, and now in academic practice—I am constantly learning new aspects of this complex business sector. The business of medicine operates as a profit-driven system where former executives from big pharma, government, and hospital C-suites work together as lobbyists, consultants, or employees of the industry. Regulations and reimbursements are the name of the game.

---

[1] "Medicine's great resignation? 1 in 5 doctors plan to exit in 2 years," AMA, January 18, 2022, https://www.ama-assn.org/practice-management/physician-health/medicine-s-great-resignation-1-5-doctors-plan-exit-2-years#:~:text=One%20in%20five%20physicians%20say,to%20recently%20published%20survey%20research.

When I attended a state regulatory public hearing in Austin in 2016, the committee on hospital regulation was meeting on perinatal regulation for the state of Texas. At the end of one of many such meetings, the chief operating officer of a prominent hospital system in Houston had a private conversation with the chairperson of the committee. Turns out they were sorority sisters in college and they were going to have dinner that evening. This is routine.

Maneuvering through the regulations and getting reimbursed for the work done can be frustrating. For example, CMS—the Centers for Medicare & Medicaid Service—changes its Medicare/Medicaid rules so frequently that you must check their website on a regular basis to be in compliance or risk being charged with billing fraud. Private insurance companies routinely adopt CMS rules. One day they will pay for a certain code and the next day they will deny payment but won't tell you why when you get the explanation of benefits. Certain procedures will require a modifier, but denial of payment will occur without a reason given. You have to figure out that a modifier is required in order for payment to be issued.

Be a Patient Advocate

The healthcare system can seem overwhelming to a new physician, but I'm going to give you some tips on how to deal with it, and perhaps even beat the powers that be at their own game.

In my specialty, I routinely have to deal with case management getting authorization for the hospital stay. Occasionally, I get a call from case management about a denial. When situations like this occur, I request a peer-to-peer review. This means I want to talk to the medical director of the insurance carrier to review the clinical facts to justify the admission. These medical directors usually have a background in a different specialty. Odds are they know nothing about neonatology.

Most of the time, the conversation is respectful and cordial. The admission is approved. Sometimes, however, it is contentious and I fail to convince the medical director to approve the authorization. When this happens, I simply inform the medical director that I disagree with their decision and that I will be documenting the entire conversation in the medical records. In my experience, most medical directors prefer to stay out of the limelight and behind the scenes. On top of that, the medical records are discoverable by legal counsel.

Here is where "office politics," or in your case, hospital politics come into play. When dealing with hospital politics, approach the situation by being a patient advocate. There are certain code words that hospitals will always pay attention to, like "patient safety" and "quality of care concerns." When you approach patient care in this way, you not only take the moral high ground, but you also become a patient advocate.

Whenever challenges or questions arise, the issue will come up during hospital committee meetings. Be prepared to attend these meetings and push the agenda up the ladder for change, always keeping your patient's care and outcomes in mind. You may encounter roadblocks from some of the older physicians who might be resistant to change. Look for allies to help champion your cause and help make changes to the quality of care in the hospital setting. These allies might include a quality control officer or risk management director. Office politics would be no different. Try to get allies or consensus—especially from the partners or senior physicians—prior to the meetings.

Using these tactics is the best way to be a patient advocate in light of many challenges and barriers from different interest groups within the healthcare industry. Change moves slowly. Keep patient care delivery and your own reputation top of mind, and don't get discouraged. The system sometimes is a game. You must be able to work within the system and not fight it.

In pediatrics, a newborn has thirty days to be added to their parent's insurance plan. So, the option is to be added to mom's insurance, dad's insurance, Medicaid, or self pay.. If the mom is not married, then the baby is assigned to the mom's insurance while in the hospital. Then, onto dad's insurance once discharged from the hospital under dad's last name. If a claim is sent in too soon or under the wrong last name, it will be denied. The payment request for a newborn admitted to the neonatal ICU can be denied if clinicals are not called to the insurance company with a denial of prior authorization code. Prior authorization has to be called into the insurance by case management to ensure that the hospitalization will get paid and reviewed by utilization review.

These types of games played by insurance companies are just the tip of the iceberg. But these are the rules you must follow if you want to get paid for services rendered. Everything they do is legal and there is nothing you can do except appeal. And if your appeal is not submitted within a certain allowable timeframe, it is considered past filing deadline and you won't get paid. Medicaid also has a time limit to submit a claim. Each insurance carrier and each state have a different time limit. So, your billing company must stay on top of these deadlines.

Physicians game the system too. There was a very successful physician who owned a hospital in Houston. They didn't participate in any managed care plans, yet they made millions legally. How did they do this? There is a loophole in CMS rules that if a patient is admitted through the emergency room, then insurances must reimburse 70% of billed charges. What does that mean? A CT scan that costs $1,000 is now $10,000. And insurances must reimburse 70% of the new charges. Physician owners in their offices would routinely refer their patients for inpatient admission through the emergency room. Of course, they must disclose that the hospital they are sending the patient to is owned by the physician, but that information is displayed at the reception desk . . . in small print. These loopholes don't last long, and regulations are constantly changing to keep up with the game on both sides. This doesn't mean all physician-owned hospitals are successful. Plenty fail. But when congress passed the Affordable Care Act (ACA) in 2010 they placed a ban any further physician-owned hospital.

I knew a physician who was fed up with the system some years ago. He had his second child in the Neonatal ICU. But his wife and child were on Medicaid. Apparently, she is officially single but lives in a million-dollar house. He obviously could have them both on his insurance but chose not to do so. His reason: because he does so much charity work in his office that he feels this is his way of taking things back. The money he saves from not having to pay for private insurance goes to the family's yearly vacation. There are also some OB doctors advertising overseas for full-service deliveries here in the United States for a certain prepaid fee to include transportation to the US with room and boarding months prior to delivery . . . all to acquire a US citizenship for the newborn. Unfortunately, this doesn't cover neonatology fees should there be any problems with the baby.

As you can imagine, there are plenty of get rich schemes and ways to scam the system. The temptation is there for many doctors, new and experienced, but believe, me physicians aren't the only ones taking advantage of the system. Regardless, please don't fall into any of it. Sooner or later the law will catch up with you.

> **Remember why you chose medicine to begin with.**

Take my word for it, you are ill-prepared for the real world of business, but you don't have to be. Essentially, you are like a newly hatched turtle making your way into the vast ocean of hope. First, you have to survive the journey across the sand, hoping to avoid getting snatched up by a seagull flying above. If you make it to the shoreline, you have to swim frantically against the current so you can reach the depths of the ocean. Once there, beware of the sharks and other snapping predators that could gobble you up in one bite. Very few of those turtles survive. Knowledge—and some luck—will help you succeed.

Don't back out now. The world needs more doctors who care, who are smart, and who are savvy. Remember why you chose medicine to begin with.

There are only a few of us dinosaurs who have survived. And we have done so because we made it from the sand to the ocean and out into the wild. Like those tiny turtles, the first steps are the most critical. Like those baby turtles, some physicians will thrive and succeed in their careers. Only a percentage get to my age and experience the level of success I have been fortunate to achieve. The others either quit, get eaten up by the system and burn out, change careers, or continue to work in the same dead-end position unfulfilled. Those physicians who remain in dead-end positions become extremely dissatisfied, bitter, angry people, a shell of the idealistic person they were when they graduated from medical school.

The business of medicine is messy. If you went into medicine to become extremely wealthy, then you don't work for anyone. Start your own business and build your own private practice. Even then, there are plenty of private practices that struggle financially to make ends meet. That's where strategy comes into play. You may want to expand the practice to a point where you become attractive to a potential buyer to buy you out. You may think they are buying your business based on your receivables. You would be wrong. They may be buying you out due to your market penetration. Think about all those free-standing urgent care/emergency room businesses. They are being bought out as hospitals try to spread their entrapment areas. To be profitable in this business venture, you would need to have substantial patient numbers and demand high dollars for services provided in order to see a significant return on investment (ROI).

In my own neonatology practice, I decided to expand the practice from one to two hospitals, not because I needed the revenue but because I recognized the changing political landscape in Houston. Hospitals were getting bought out. Small neonatal practices like mine were being replaced by bigger, more established groups. I had to get bigger and fast. I also had to offer better services than these bigger groups. It wasn't that I had better doctors or better outcomes. Rather, I was able to keep higher acuity patients and thus higher reimbursements for the hospital. Remember that it's a cost center for hospitals. I was also able to offer my services at a cheaper price compared to bigger organizations. My overhead was significantly lower than bigger groups with much higher administrative overhead. Once I had accomplished this, I was able to under bid for the contract. The hospitals had little incentive to change neonatal groups, unless it was politically motivated. Politics always involves relationships. Once I had achieved significant volume with hospital contracts, my group had better leverage in negotiating managed care contracts.

So, when I decided to sell my practice, it wasn't about my total revenues or total account receivables. Some of my hospital contracts were in Medicaid-only hospitals. It was about market share and market penetration. During the negotiations, I told the chief negotiator that in five years, I had increased my market share in Dallas from 0% to 25% of the market. "In the next five years, if you don't buy us out, we will expand our market share to 40% in Dallas," I said. I told him we were in direct talks with two other hospitals that had contracts with his group. He didn't hesitate to agree to terms after that.

Heed the advice in this book and learn the business before starting your own practice. But you have to start somewhere, and this book is a great jumping off point.

Consider yourself in the minor leagues heading into the major leagues. How you enter the game and manage those years in the minors can determine how you succeed when you get called up to the majors. There is a role for doctors who just want to take care of patients nine to five. There's a role for doctors who want to be leaders in their field. There's also a role for doctors who want to be entrepreneurs. You have to be in the right practice to be the leader you want to be. Just as important as being in the right place is starting off on the right foot. And that begins with having the right relationships, understanding the politics, and foremost, knowing who you are.

NEW PHYSICIAN, KNOW THYSELF

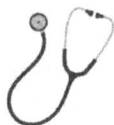

One of the best pieces of advice I can give you is to know yourself. Of course, you think you know who you are, but do you really?

Who are you? Really, who are you as an individual? This might sound like a meaningless question, but it isn't. Your self-definition impacts your priorities, your goals, and your behaviors (both personal and professional). When you understand who you are, you bring that to the negotiation table as a new physician. So, how do you determine who you are? I'm not talking about what makes a good habit or a magnetic personality for a physician. Your self-definition is something that you, and only you, will need to find out. The answer won't come to you immediately. Some people never arrive at an answer to this question. Some of us discover who we are after a period of roaming the desert. Take some time to ponder this question, keeping in mind that you may change as you get older or further in your career.

Determine what's important to you personally, work/life balance versus your professional status. Maybe both hold an equally important place on your list of priorities. In this case, you will have to keep balance front and center in your life. Managing that balance will be difficult, but it is possible. You will have to make some tough choices, like declining a particular job offer if you know it will interfere with your family life, or skipping a few of your child's events in order to tend to patient emergencies. You get to choose. Just remember that things change constantly, and you hold the power to make the choices that benefit you. Be willing to give up some things in order to get what you ultimately want. Make sure your significant other understands and appreciates what you are trying to accomplish. Similarly, your partner should be involved in and agree with your short-term and long-term career goals.

As a new graduate, you have been through years of delayed gratification. Unlike your peers who have pursued other fields of study that allowed free time, the opportunity to engage in hobbies, and the option to work in their city of choice, you chose a career that places you at the mercy of the system, at least in the beginning. However, even as you might feel that your options are limited, you do still have options, and those options are guided, first and foremost, by your priorities today and your goals for your future.

As you advance in your career and start to understand the business of medicine, you will be better able to do the following:

- Define Your Career Goals
- Explore Your Priorities
- Establish Your Personal Brand and Ethics
- Know Your Self-Worth

Define Your Career Goals

Why did you choose medicine as a career? Really explore that question. Your reason for choosing your career path is yours alone, so you might as well admit it. Was it to save lives, heal the world, make your parents proud, or outshine a sibling or best friend? My decision to apply to medical school was influenced by my physician dad. He was a doctor of obstetrics and gynecology and couldn't understand why

I didn't want to follow in his footsteps in "the world's greatest spe-ciality," according to him. At least I was going to work with obste-tricians as a pediatrician, I told him. He didn't talk to me for two weeks. Despite that, I stayed true to my interests, and so should you.

Did you choose a career in medicine to get rich? If so, I hate to tell you, but you just wasted fourteen years of your life. There are many other ways to get rich in a much shorter time and for far less cost than the academic hell you just completed. Just look at the many Tik-Tokers or the YouTubers making millions. I'm not saying you can't get extremely wealthy being a physician. You can definitely be financially secure and even be a millionaire, but you'll be working long hours for someone or for a company for the rest of your life in order to be financially secure.

You will need to be your own boss and diversify your business interests or hold shares in your own company to be a wealthy physician. In fact, many private practices include other income revenue streams that have nothing to do with their specialty. For example, some private medical practices use real estate holdings to grow their wealth. They will buy land and develop it as a strip mall, then house a medical office there as an anchor business. As the practice grows its revenues, they might open another medical office in a different part of town, purchasing land once again. Now, they have built equity in the real estate as well as in the practice. Another strategy is to open after-hours clinics—like pain or sleep labs—as a side businesses, essentially diversifying revenue for greater profits. That's how you get rich! As with any other business venture, having multiple revenue streams is an important strategy for growing wealth.

Exit strategy is an important part of any business. During the COVID-19 pandemic, 43% of physicians changed jobs, 8% retired, and 3% left medicine to pursue non-clinical careers, according to a CHG healthcare survey in 2022.[2] Their biggest motivation for making a change in career was a better work/life balance. Physicians at different stages of their career had different motivations for their career change. Early-career physicians (less than 10 years) were motivated by a more desirable location. Mid-career physicians (10 to 20 years) were more interested in better workplace culture. And late-career physicians (greater than 20 years) were motivated by more flexibility in location and how often to work. Overall, the top concerns during the pandemic were poor leadership, lack of employer support, and insufficient staffing levels. These are all issues that have been longstanding yet were exacerbated by the pandemic.

If you haven't already given it some thought, now is the perfect time to consider what your career goals are. Write down your short-term goals for the next three to five years. Those goals might look something like this:

- Pass the national board certification
- Manage stress
- Attract and retain more patients
- Increase salary
- Improve work/life balance
- Better understand the business of medicine

Now, what are your longer-term goals of ten to twenty years? Write them down. Maybe they include something like:

- Job security
- Family
- Financial security

---

[2] "Survey: Nearly half of physicians changed jobs during the pandemic," CHC Healthcare, June 27, 2022, https://chghealthcare.com/blog/physicians-changed-jobs-survey

- Owning or starting a business
- Professional recognition

Do you want time flexibility or career visibility? Do you see yourself as head of a department at a large hospital or leading a dedicated team in a small private practice? Or, do you want to have a family and settle down with kids? Any of the options is possible; you just have to know what you want as you progress in your career and life.

I was full of excitement with my first real job at that national medical group based in Florida. But I was disappointed with what happened. When I finally left that role—minus the $20,000 for tail malpractice insurance I later learned I didn't actually have to purchase—I was a bit battered and bruised. I licked my wounds and moved on in search of a new practice. A smaller practice, perhaps? Something closer to my hometown of Spartanburg, South Carolina. That search sent me to Savannah, Georgia where I joined a private practice. Months after joining the practice, I learned that the nurses had a betting pool to guess how long I would last. The previous physician was there a mere two years before resigning. Would I do any better? After my previous employment experience, I was determined to be smarter with this one.

Deciding to do some recognizance on this practice, I called and spoke with one of the physicians, who told me that everything was good there. He had left because he'd received a job offer he couldn't refuse. *Okay, that sounds feasible.* He didn't let on about any problems with the practice or the partners, and I believed him. But had I ignored the red flags again? I soon discovered that the practice had a bad record with physician retention. There had been a revolving door with physicians coming and going for years, but I didn't bother to ask about the longevity of the physicians at the practice. Only the nurses were able to tell me this . . . after I had already signed the contract.

After three years it became apparent that I would never become a partner in this practice, despite the many promises that I could. The first clue was during one of my last performance evaluations. Although I received acclaim for my patient advocacy and clinical skill, one of the partners had written in an evaluation that people had trouble understanding my English because of my accent. I was floored. I grew up in Spartanburg, South Carolina. What accent? Then, the previous physician called me out of the blue and told me the real reasons why he had left the practice and suggested that I should consider leaving too. When we previously spoke, he had been under a gag clause in his contract not to say anything negative about the practice. By this time, that order had expired so he was able to speak freely about that medical group. He didn't share anything clinical or business related, but he did let on that no one else was going to make partnership. It had become quite evident to me that the partners were trying to push me through that revolving door. I decided to follow his advice and resign after my third year.

Soon after leaving that medical group in Savannah, I was offered a new position at another hospital in South Carolina as the neonatologist at a Level-2 nursery responsible for developing their program. In this new position, my goals changed. I brought my previous knowledge to bear and decided to put my all into building a world-class neonatology program from scratch. My goal now was to demonstrate my clinical excellence and prove that I could develop a program that was second to none.

The first day on the job, I met with the chief of OB. In casual conversation, he asked where I grew up. When I told him South Carolina he was surprised and said he was told that people couldn't understand my accent. He laughed and said, "Son, you're one of us with that Southern accent." With that, I felt welcomed, a much different experience than at my previous employer that was looking for a way to get rid of me. It was at this new hospital that I learned how cutthroat and dirty the business of medicine can be.

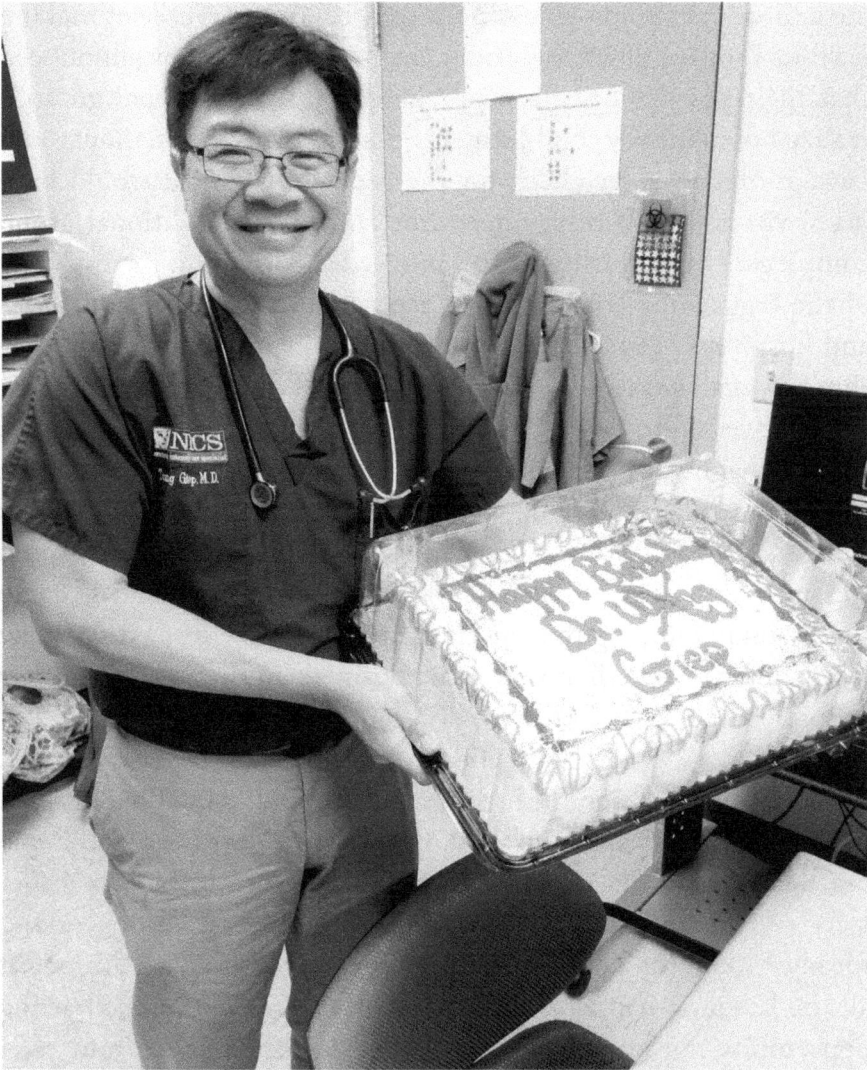

First day at a hospital in Texarkana. They thought I was Dr Wong.
Not even my birthday.

Within days of starting this new program, the larger practice across town called me in for a meeting and offered me an opportunity to join their private practice. "This sounds interesting," I said. "Make me an offer I can't refuse." They offered me a three-year employment package with no guarantee of making partner. I turned down their offer. Six months later, they announced that their practice had been purchased by a big national group. I realized then that by combining my practice with theirs, they would have gotten a bigger check for the acquisition, and I would have been without a job soon afterward. Once the big national group completed the acquisition, they proceeded to acquire the majority of the bigger nurseries, forming a powerful coalition of nurseries and hospital systems. They then petitioned the state legislature to shut down all smaller nurseries in the name of quality and patient safety. Overnight, I went from a bustling nursery to being empty, from managing sick newborns to writing Op-Eds for newspapers, and going to state regulatory meetings. Soon, new regulations were adopted in favor of bigger nurseries. My time at this hospital was up. With all of this upheaval, I realized that I had become successful in building this program. I was a threat. But I didn't take it personally. After all, it was smart business on their part. Another lesson learned for the future.

By now, I was getting the hang of this business of medicine and my entire future vision for my career changed. I knew I had to look out for myself first. I found an opportunity to start my own private practice in Houston, Texas. This was my chance to build another Level-2 nursery and to be an entrepreneur. At least I'd be working for myself, not for a boss as an employee. It was scary, but I brought all the lessons I had learned in South Carolina and jumped at the opportunity, not really knowing what I had gotten myself into.

As it turned out, the pediatricians at this hospital had all left due to a major malpractice loss. One of the pediatricians had been sued for malpractice because a baby born prematurely and transferred to a tertiary center had been diagnosed with cerebral palsy. The case went on to a trial by jury. This is extremely rare. Most cases get settled before a trial. As the courtroom drama played out, the lawyers for the family called the pediatrician to the witness stand.

"How many resuscitations did you do this month?" the attorney asked.

The pediatrician responded, "I am national resuscitation provider certified."

"That is not the question," the attorney replied. "Please answer the question."

Her answer: "None."

The attorney then asked, "How many did you do last year?"

Her reply was the same; none.

"How many did you do this past couple of years?"

Again, her answer was zero.

The attorney then turned to the jury and asked, "Is this the most qualified person to resuscitate your child?"

The jury deliberated and decided for the family, awarding a multi-million-dollar judgement. This forced the hospital to search for a neonatologist. That's where I came in.

When I shared with my dad my excitement that I was moving to Texas, he made no effort to hide his disappointment. I was surprised and shocked.

"Why Texas, of all places?" he asked as if I'd said I was moving to Mars.

I pondered the question, searching his face for some indication of the source of his discontent. "Well, this is a great offer, and I don't think I can afford to pass it up." After all, it was a new start and a chance to start my own private practice, my own business, to be an entrepreneur.

In that moment, I felt I needed to sell him on the idea, even though the decision was mine, one hundred percent. I explained to him what I had learned with the previous jobs I'd had, the difficulties I had run into with not being able to make partner, being bamboozled into buying insurance, and even the subtle bigotry of people suggesting they couldn't understand me when I spoke. My goals had shifted. I no longer wanted to work for someone else.

Now, I was ready to start my own business. I had no one else to consider except myself, so I felt ready to be a business owner and an entrepreneur.

What he told me next stayed with me my entire career. "Maybe the problem wasn't those jobs or people," he said, raising one eyebrow as he stared deeply into my eyes. "Have you looked into a mirror? Maybe the problem is you."

That was my "Gone with Wind" Scarlett O'Hara moment. Remember when Scarlett swore to god that she would never be poor again? This was my moment and my eventual motivation not to fail . . . at any cost. In retrospect, my dad wasn't entirely wrong. I didn't know what it meant to own a business or to be an entrepreneur. Even after six years in the medical profession, I still didn't entirely know the business of medicine. I was still testing the waters, searching for someone else's measure of success, uncertain of my true goals in medicine. I discovered that what I learned during my training only applied to the clinical part of my career. The business side came later and was a lot more complicated than I could ever imagine. I was only beginning to grasp the concept of the business of medicine. Despite all the setbacks with the previous three positions I'd held, there were more setbacks and lessons I needed to learn. Understanding how billing and collections work, having a firm grasp of the CPT codes, insurance reimbursement, and managed care contracts and terminology. I still didn't know the intricacies of human resource laws and regulations, federal and state laws and Medicaid regulations, or the intricacies of hospital politics.

Along with all of these blind spots, I needed to differentiate my neonatology practice from others. So, I sought counsel from my dad's business consultant to help set up my private practice. We spent many hours talking about business and its challenges. I learned as much about business from him as he learned from me about my specialty. With his help, I finally understood what a hospital wants. Initially, I thought they wanted clinical excellence. In part, they do, but that's not all. Every physician can deliver and run a tight ship. Above all, though, the CEO of a hospital lives or dies on the bottom line: profit. A hospital is a business and it has to answer to corporate and other executives. Above all they want to be profitable, and the neonatal ICU is a cost center to the hospital.

The CEO of a hospital has to deal with different doctors from different specialties, from surgeons to internists. Every physician complains to the CEO and wants more for their department, otherwise, they won't refer their patients to that hospital. Most CEOs understand surgical services, and that is often who they cater to. But babies are like a foreign concept. Labor and delivery don't generate a lot of revenue, and typically lose money for a hospital. Depending on the payer mix, those areas might even be a negative profit center. But the neonatal ICU makes a lot of money. Neonatology is like the little engine that could. Knowing this, I learned to educate the hospital administrator on the value of having a Level-2 or Level-3 ICU. From using the correct codes for level of acuity, to building the ancillary personnel, to the equipment necessary to function at a higher level.

Most managers have never heard of InterQual criteria for critical care. They were written for adult and pediatric care. InterQual criteria are used by managed care and compliance to ensure proper coding. It is long and boring, but educational. I recommend you spend some time reading it to get a better understanding of hospital-based billing. Babies that were being billed at Level-2 charges were actually qualifying for higher acuity charges based on InterQual criteria. Managed care negotiators also routinely discount neonatal services in lieu of surgical services for higher reimbursement, much to the detriment of their bottom line. Hospital administrators routinely are not aware of these facts.

Once, I did an evaluation for a hospital and asked for the admission log for their Level-2 ICU. To my surprise, they didn't have one. I asked about the revenue for their Level-2 ICU. They didn't bill for any ICU codes since they were not a higher acuity center. Knowing that they are not a designated cardiac center, I asked if they would give anti-clotting medication to patients and bill for all related services. Of course they would. "So why wouldn't you bill for stabilization of a critically ill newborn prior to transport?" I asked. The room went silent. After that meeting, they began billing for all allowable charges, turning a negative profit center into a positive profit center. That experience demonstrated to me what I brought to the table. Beyond my clinical expertise, I offer my ability to analyze a unit and offer informed recommendations to transform it into a profitable unit while educating the administrators. These skills are not taught in clinical training; this comes with experience.

Not everyone can achieve this level of expertise, but you can when you decide on what your goals are and how to achieve them. Maybe your goal is to be a great clinician. Maybe it's to be a business owner. Maybe it's to be a partner in a business. Whatever your goals are, you need to understand them, determine how to get there, and then set your priorities to accomplish them.

Explore Your Priorities

Priorities are the measure of what matters to you now. As you consider your priorities, think about your life, your character, the people you love, your interests, and what you want for your future. Priorities change over time, and that's okay. But you must know what is important to you today. Choosing the right options for your future requires that you determine what's important to you in life. What do you want in your career? How do you define or measure success? What's more important: family, money, or something else? If you are married, you also need to consider your spouse's priorities and goals. And if you think that's not important, think again.

I knew of one physician whose first job was a perfect fit for her professionally. The hours were great, the work was satisfying, and the income was exceptional. Unfortunately, her husband was miserable in his job. Soon, the stress began to impact their relationship and family and they had to make a difficult decision. Should one spouse suffer in an unfulfilling job just so the other could enjoy career satisfaction? Of course not. My physician friend chose her marriage and decided to give up that perfect job. The couple moved to a new city where they both found fulfilling employment and were able to balance their personal and family goals so they could enjoy life. In this instance, family was a high priority.

I knew of another physician whose priorities were missionary work in Haiti, where she had adopted a child. She needed a block of time off to visit her adopted child in Haiti. Money was not important to her, but her missionary work and her adopted child were her focus. Having a schedule of two weeks on and two weeks off gave her that flexibility.

At every stage of your career, you have to be well aware of what is important to you. If you are not firmly committed to your priorities, your employer or others who influence you will project their priorities onto you. Imagine the disastrous and unfulfilling life this could result in. Don't let this happen to you. It is worth it to set aside time in your schedule regularly—once or twice a year—to assess your interests, goals, and priorities, understanding that they will change over time.

> **As you create your personal brand as a physician, you must remember that your choices matter.**

There are numerous resources online, in life planning books, and through life coaches and therapists that can help you clarify your priorities. Access these resources often. If you are already practicing, find a mentor who can help you balance the work/life experience. After all, not everyone outside of medicine understands what you had to go through to get where you are.

Establish Your Personal Brand and Ethics

When legendary NFL quarterback Tom Brady of the New England Patriots gave his acceptance speech at his induction into the National Football League Hall of Fame, he hit the nail on the head about success: "To be successful at anything, the truth is you don't have to be special. You just have to be what most people aren't: consistent, determined, and willing to work for it. No shortcuts." He then proceeded to credit the grounds crew, the equipment crew, the team doctors, and his teammates for making him successful. Throughout his twenty-three-year football career, Brady created a personal brand that became synonymous with hard work and excellence.

As you create your personal brand as a physician, you must remember that your choices matter. You are now viewed as a pillar of the community you serve. As a doctor, you are expected to be intelligent, knowledgeable, available, courteous, self-assured, confident, communicative, authoritative, reliable, and all-knowing. This means that the community you help uplift as a pillar is watching you. They expect a high level of character, behavior, decision-making, approachability, and integrity. That's a lot to live up to. But you are also human with emotions, interests, and desires apart from your role as a physician. That's what most people don't consider when they view you as a doctor. But as with any other brand, the impression is left to those who view the brand. This means that you will always have to consider how others view you. Maintain the power over your brand by choosing to determine the image you wish to project.

Market yourself for the future. What do you want to be known for or known as? What do you want people to say about you when your name comes up in a room you're not even in? How do you want to be remembered when you leave one job and go to the next? Do you want to be known as a good clinician, a stable family person, a focused individual, an honest colleague? You get to decide your personal brand and how you exude it. Doing so takes time, but once you establish your goals and your priorities, half the work is done.

With that, you just walk the talk. Sure, it'll take time to find your mojo, but once you do, it will become a natural part of who you are. You create a set of actions that demonstrate who you say you are and how you want to be viewed by others.

Your personal brand extends beyond your person; it also extends to your employer's brand. Once you make any career choice, you need to be in it one hundred percent. Think of it as if you just joined the military: You're in the army now! You are officially part of the brand of that employer, and they expect you to represent them in all aspects, on and off the clock. This includes how you speak to and behave with colleagues, patients, vendor representatives, and community members. Every action you take reflects the image of the brand you represent, your employer's and your own.

Throughout my career as a physician working for private practices and hospital groups, and having employed more than 150 staff in my own private practice, I have seen the good and the bad of where personal branding and ethics intersect. From office romances and issuing questionable prescriptions to patients, to unnecessary surgeries and billing and financial improprieties. Anything done under questionable ethics will always come to light. Don't be on the dark side of ethics. Begin now to establish and continuously develop a personal brand that reflects the highest professional ethics. But you must separate ethics and personal brand. Ethics is expected of us all, but a personal brand is unique to you.

Medical schools don't teach you how to behave in professional settings. You might have had one or two courses on ethics each year. Those mandatory courses might have touched on the rights of the patient and hospital/office staff, as well as the four pillars of medical ethics:

1. Autonomy. Respect for a patient's right to self-determination.
2. Beneficence. Duty to do good.
3. Non-maleficence. Duty to not to do bad.
4. Justice. To treat all people equally and equitably.

These only scratched the surface of the ethical issues you will encounter as a physician.

With every decision you make, you define your personal brand and how it will affect your credibility and your ability to advance in your career. Sure, you have a life of your own, but when you sign on to work for someone, your brand is now part of their brand, like it or not. Over time, you should be able to distinguish yourself and add your unique brand to your employer's brand. Your brand can be almost anything from being good with patients to being on time.

Here are some top traits of a good physician that will help you stay focused on your career. You may discover more as you advance in your career.

1. Getting things done. Learn to focus. That is a 24/7 job. Physicians tend to get a lot of paperwork piling up on our desk, from lab reports to correspondence. Be organized and do one thing at a time, then move on to the next thing. Don't procrastinate. Develop a system to handle the paperwork.

2. Being aware of your abilities and limitations. A good physician knows their weaknesses and their strengths. Don't be afraid to ask for consultations or too proud to ask for help. Don't wing it.

3. Treating everyone with respect, especially the patients, staff, colleagues, and non-medical personnel. Get to know and greet housekeeping and unit secretaries by name. When you treat them with respect you will earn their respect in return.

4. Explaining things so that laypeople can understand. Speak slowly and simplify difficult topics, but don't dumb it down too much. For example, when explaining complex congenital cyanotic heart disease, I usually talk about plumbing. The heart being the pump, and the arteries and veins being PVC

pipes carrying water back to the pump. Congenital heart disease is simply plumbing with the wrong pipe connections.

5. Handling stress or conflict well. Don't freak out. Be calm and in control. Take a deep breath and concentrate. Systematically handle one thing at a time, whether it be paperwork or dealing with a difficult patient or family. In the midst of a potentially hostile or difficult situation, I would step out of the room, take a deep breath, and take a moment to compose myself before walking back in.

6. Accepting and embracing change. Be willing to embrace change, whether that is changes to the staff, relocation, or even the introduction of technology. In full honesty, I miss the days of paper charting, but I appreciate the efficiency of electronic medical records.

7. Being able to communicate clearly and effectively. Avoid being confusing or contradictory when speaking with colleagues and staff. I would routinely stop the conversation and ask, "Please tell me what you heard me say." Conversely, I would tell others, "This is what I hear you saying." These statements during a conversation help eliminate misunderstandings between the parties.

8. Managing time well. Get into a routine that works for you. Complete documentation in a timely fashion. Handle the flow of patients to be seen. I have seen colleagues with the same volume of patients as myself spend double the time charting. Perhaps you spend too much time chatting on the phone or with colleagues. Maybe you enjoy scanning the internet or social media or researching topics or even golfing. None of this is bad, but it could interfere with your primary functions as a physician. Identify your time-wasters and minimize them as much as possible.

9. Being open to criticism. This is always a tough one. No one is perfect. Admit that you will make mistakes, that you don't know everything, and that the way you do things is not the only way or the right way. Accept constructive criticism from those with more experience than you have and be willing to adjust your thinking and your actions when you have new information.

10. Being available. When the hospital or answering service calls you at 3:00 a.m., you promptly answer the phone. You are in a life-or-death career. That's just part of the job. Above all, do not get angry when they call you by mistake.

Some other areas where doctors get into trouble with ethics involve questionable behavior. Office/hospital gossip is common in any profession. Avoid it at all costs. Becoming the topic of gossip might be less in your control, but being the originator of the gossip is certainly something you can avoid. Be respectful of the character and personal lives of those you work with. No one wants their reputation ruined by office/hospital gossip. A reputation is easy to destroy and even harder to repair.

Office/hospital romances are extremely hard to keep quiet and even harder when you're married. Improper romances are enough of a stressor for the people involved. Add to that the decision an employer is forced to make once the romance is exposed, and you have a recipe for disaster. Which employee should the employer keep: the physician or the other staff member? Don't ever make your employer choose between keeping you or someone else on staff. Even if you are the one who remains, the poor reputation you have created—which includes being the cause of someone else losing their job—will be forever remembered by others.

Or imagine this: A physician gets called into the emergency department (ED) for a consultation. The ED staff smells alcohol, and the physician is slurring his speech. He admits he's had a few drinks. We all know that this issue will be brought to the medical executive meeting and evaluated for possible impaired physician. Whatever the outcome, it won't be in the best interest of the physician's brand in the long run. Don't let this happen to you. Be mindful of your consumption of legal substances like alcohol. As for illegal substances, just don't do it. Some hospital bylaws allow for random drug testing, and employer contracts may also stipulate the same. State medical boards are still very conservative. Marijuana may be legal in some states, but the medical boards and medical executives of hospitals are still very conservative and do not allow this among physicians.

Email is as much a part of life these days as breathing. Most people assume the cover of privacy with emails, but your electronic communications are one of the first places investigators will look for evidence when your conduct is in question. Be careful with emails, especially business emails. They are all discoverable. Do you think deleting them will protect you? Think again. Those emails can be recovered. Do not communicate anything on public or hospital computers that could cause your reputation to be at stake. Text messages on company phones are treated the same as emails. Remember what happened to Hillary Clinton's server and BlackBerry phone. She bleached the emails and took a hammer to her BlackBerry, but the emails were saved and discovered on a different server.

As with email, social media is a normal part of life and a common way people communicate. Similarly, social media posts are not private and are discoverable. Therefore, do not post images or opinions or make incriminating comments on social media that you don't want anyone to see or read. It doesn't matter if it's shared only among friends and family or that it was intended as a joke. Let your private life remain private and keep your political views to yourself. As a physician, you are now a pillar of society, not that fun-loving student you were in medical school. Speaking of your life as a student, your social media profiles are part of your resumé. It is common for employers to look at a potential new hire's social media. Similarly, patients and their families can find you on social media. I've had plenty of parents and grandparents who have looked up my Facebook page. Nurses and other colleagues are not exempted from doing the same. Although you cannot scrub your social media accounts of every post you have ever made, you can go forward demonstrating the professional you desire to be. Therefore, from this day forth, be mindful of what you post on social media.

Just as important as not expressing controversial or questionable views on social media, it is important to demonstrate some positive aspects of your personality. In short, don't be boring. Have some depth that shows your interests. Things like family, travel, hobbies, and volunteer interests are particularly beneficial in portraying yourself as a well-rounded candidate. Just be sure what you reveal is truthful and authentic.

Post-COVID, the view of the medical community has shifted. Patients and families are consulting "Dr. Google" and doing internet searches on certain medical problems and coming up with different diagnoses. It's like in the movie *Kindergarten Cop* when Arnold Schwarzenegger's character complained about having a headache and one of his kindergarten students responded, "Maybe it's a tumor." Physicians are no longer the only source of medical knowledge. However, experienced analysis and judgement will become much more important in day-to-day medical situations.

Know Your Self-Worth

Most people think of self-worth as relating to your job, the value you bring to your workplace, coworkers, and patients as illustrated by your income. But it's much more than that. Self-worth is the value you place on yourself as a person. This is not defined by the income you earn or the praise you receive from others. Nor is it diminished by the mistakes you make, complaints you receive from patients, or not getting the promotion you worked so hard for.

Self-worth is an inside job. It is something you have to work on over years. It is the value and importance you place on yourself, your character, abilities, insights, knowledge, compassion, intellect, and more. As you develop as an adult and a medical professional, you will begin to place a value on certain characteristics of thought and behavior. You might notice that a colleague exemplifies integrity in each interaction with others, and you want to embody that same integrity. You value that and work to emulate it. Or you might find that your compassionate approach to patients adds to your enjoyment of the work you do, so you lean into that. Or you may take pride in your insistence that your employer respect your time off so you can focus on your family, mental health, and overall enjoyment of life. Each of these things and more adds to your self-worth. As you begin your career, be aware of the factors that impact your self-worth. Make the commitment to enhance and expand what really matters to you so that as your career evolves, so does your self-worth.

Looking back at my career, I wish I'd had a mentor to teach me the business and the pitfalls of this profession. When I started out, I had the necessary training to be a great clinician, but I didn't have the business or organizational skills needed to run a business. Honestly, I didn't even know I needed that insight. I was lucky in learning from the family business consultant as well as a friendly CEO who helped guide me on the business side. But from where I stand now, I know that every physician needs to know the business side of medicine, not just the clinical side. Everything I learned, I learned through failure. Failure is not the end, but a lesson to learn from. I now know how billing and collections work: how to get paid by the insurance companies; how much to write off; what games insurance and billing companies play; how hospitals get paid; and how the hospital billing and collections works.

There is also a fine line between knowing your self-worth and being cocky or arrogant. I once had a physician interviewing for a position with my organization. He wanted to be paid the same amount as I was being paid. I asked, "What makes you worth that much salary?" He couldn't justify it. But I gave him an A+ for effort and ingenuity. Warning: Don't try this technique with employers.

Many physicians I know wouldn't take the first step to become an entrepreneur or risk a partnership with someone. I get it; it's scary and comes with a lot of risk. Would I do it all over again knowing what I know today? Absolutely. Would I change anything? Indeed, I would. But overall, I wouldn't change my goals. Everything I've learned over time came from the multitude of mistakes I made during my career.

Would pursuing an MBA have prepared me for my role as a business owner? Maybe, maybe not. I'm not sure it would have helped me as an entrepreneur or even as a business owner. It would definitely not have helped me deal with the politics I encountered. I'm not saying an MBA isn't a valuable degree. Having it would have helped me climb the corporate ladder. It would have helped me understand spreadsheets and talk with accountants, but not with the day-to-day operations. Even in the principles of negotiations, I learned my own approach to a BATNA (Best Alternative to a Negotiated Agreement). I've been told by my family business consultant that I am one of the best natural negotiators he has ever met in his career. Sure, I could have learned the principles of negotiation in an MBA program, but nothing beats being in a real-life negotiation and going to bat for yourself and winning. Watching the body language of the person across the table and knowing your opposition. I'll share more about negotiation strategies later on in the book.

At this point in your career, you won't have much to leverage in negotiations, so stick with areas you can reach an agreement on, like salary, time, and lifestyle.

Life After Medicine

As doctors, we dedicate our lives to helping save the lives of others. The sad thing is, once we reach the pinnacle of success, we don't know anything else. Is there life after medicine? You might not want to think about that right now, as you begin your medical career. But this question is crucial to knowing who you are, why you do what you do, the kind of person you want to become, and where you want to be in your life. Your medical career will end. You might as well think now about what that end could look like and design your pathway toward it rather than waiting until the end is staring you in the face and you are ill-prepared for it. Have an exit strategy. Develop hobbies and other interests. My dad didn't retire from OB until he was eighty years old because his medical career was all he knew.

After I sold my practice, I thought I would retire. That lasted five months. I thought traveling the world would be my new gig. But that got old quickly and became quite costly. There's no better place than home. I developed hobbies and took on a new challenge in my current position working for a children's hospital, developing a telemedicine program, and running the children's community hospital nursery programs.

What I have realized is that there will be some important innovations in medicine as the 21st century evolves. This is an exciting time to be in medicine. New medications and devices are coming to market at a breakneck pace. Artificial intelligence is quickly taking hold and will assist doctors in our daily routine, perhaps with our diagnoses or even with an Electronic Medical Record (EMR). As I mentioned earlier, AI is already answering medical questions that patients have. AI is also revolutionizing the front office with virtual receptionists as well as a virtual answering service. The use of Dr. Google or WebMD has challenged our medical knowledge by allowing patients to check the validity of what physicians recommend. The acceptance of telemedicine will give much-needed access to medical care in rural areas without doctors having to travel, thereby limiting physician burnout. This is one of the strategies outlined by AMA to avoid physician burnout.

Now that I am in the late phase of my career, I can look back at my life and see what I did wrong and what I would have done differently. My biggest regret is not being able to find someone to take over and run the business I created as it needed to be run. I view it as similar to the struggle of Steve Jobs at Apple. He was the inspiration and the heart of Apple. The company was nothing without him. To find that one person who has the same vision for the company as you do is one of the most challenging things for a founder. I was never able to find that person, even though all my doctors felt they were qualified to run the practice themselves. But business is all about relationships, no matter what business you are in. Not many people understand that. It's also about the ability to negotiate and leverage your position. If I had found the ideal person to take over my practice, it would have allowed me to spend more time with my family. This was my biggest regret in my career.

I mention all of this to say, you are a person first, a human being. That means there are other concerns and priorities in your life even as you grow within your career (or, at least, there should be). As a new physician coming out of training, you need to learn how to get started and not become jaded by the system. I'm going to give you a head start on understanding how to handle your first job and get through the hurdles of the first three years in your career. So, pay close attention . . . and keep your fingers crossed.

EMPLOYMENT OPTIONS AND THE JOB INTERVIEW: QUESTIONS, EXPECTATIONS, AND RED FLAGS

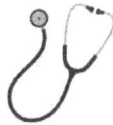

A s you approach graduation and get ready to enter your dream career as a medical professional, you have many options for employment. Every physician's job search begins with a curriculum vitae (CV) or resumé. As a recent resident, your CV should focus primarily on your medical education and training and include the following key information:

- Name and contact information
- Date and place of birth, and citizenship
- Education, including undergraduate and residency training
- Current and past licenses, active and nonactive, or application status
- Current board certifications or application status
- Experience related to the medical field
- Any applicable publications

- Memberships in professional associations and committees
- Awards and honors
- Board certifications
- Hobbies

Your CV represents a snapshot of you up to this point. It is your introduction to a potential employer. You want to look good and ensure that all information is accurate. Never, ever lie or embellish your accomplishments. If writing isn't your strong suit, consider hiring a professional writer or utilizing a CV website that specializes in healthcare to ensure yours is polished and professional.

As a medical resident or recent grad, you have several tools at your disposal to save time and streamline the search process. The internet is a good place to start. Online healthcare career centers like Health eCareers (*healthecareers.com*) offer more than just job listings. You will also find useful information on industry trends, best practices for applications, resumes and interviews, and salary ranges for certain types of physicians. You can also work with a healthcare recruiter who is skilled in making the match between employer and candidate. Many hospitals and healthcare systems have in-house recruiting teams as well. So, if there is a company in a specific location where you want to work, reach out directly. Even if there is nothing available right now, they can keep your CV on file for future opportunities.

There are also physician search firms that do the work for you. Most recruitment firms charge the employer a flat fee once you sign a contract. That flat fee, which can run upwards of several thousand dollars, can make you less attractive to employers when it comes time to hire. Also, because there is a commission at stake, third-party firms can sometimes pressure candidates to decide before they are ready. Therefore, enter these arrangements carefully and after some serious thought.

Your colleagues and mentors are also valuable assets in your quest for your first physician job after residency. Talk to previous graduates from your alma mater. You will be surprised at how important your professional network will be as you grow in your role as a physician. Having peers to bounce ideas off of and lean on for support is vital for those working in such a high-pressure sector. Expand your network by attending department meetings and professional conferences, joining professional associations, and working with a mentor who can connect you with other providers. Get comfortable telling others that you have completed your residency and you are looking for a new position. Strong professional networking is sometimes the most promising way to find a new job. And don't forget to pay it forward once you are hired. Look out for your colleagues, help them connect to other physicians, and recommend them for a position with your employer if you think they'd be a good fit.

Your Employment Options

There are a multitude of career options for you to explore as a new physician. Consider what you read in the previous chapter as you make your decision. Your goals, priorities, personal brand, and self-worth are highly influential in making the right choice for your first job. You have paid your dues on the academic side; now it's time to learn your craft, practice your skills, and enter medical practice with your eyes wide open.

As you progress in your career, you might want to earn more money. At some point, you might consider earning an MBA and going into the corporate side of medicine. Or, like me, you might wish to stretch your entrepreneurial muscles as founder of your own private practice. Whatever choice you make as a physician, the organization you join is a business and will be run as a business. Never lose sight of that.

For now, here are a few options for employment that you should be aware of:

- Hospital
- HMO
- Corporate
- Private Practice
- Academic Medicine
- Locum Tenens
- Graduate Studies
- Military

Hospital

Employment is usually published on the hospital or health system website. Often recruiters will reach out via email or text. Physicians are usually W-2 employees of the hospital or health system. You focus on patient care. Salary and benefits are guaranteed. There is no financial risk. The administrative functions are handled by the hospital or health system. Just like any organization, there is a hierarchy and bureaucracy. There is always a risk of getting lost in the system or overlooked, despite your skill and accomplishments. The administrator may not have experience running your practice and may oversee multiple practices. It's important to have an experienced physician working with that administrator to help guide the practice.

HMO

A Health Maintenance Organization (HMO) is an organization or network that provides health insurance coverage for a monthly or annual fee. The HMO requires primary care physicians to refer patients and has constrained physician networks. In other words, you can only refer patients to physicians within the network and not outside the network unless you have prior authorization. This is how they are able to control the costs. There are four models of HMO practices:

Group model. A single person in charge, making all the decisions and taking all the risks associated with the business.

Individual physician association (IPA). A group of independent practices joining together as part of the HMO practice. They are loosely affiliated. Each group functions independently except for the business side. IPAs are usually formed to negotiate better reimbursement with insurances.

Network model. Network HMO usually contracts with several independent providers or groups of specialists to provide certain medical services. These contractors can see non-HMO members.

Staff model. Kaiser is an example of the staff model HMO. Kaiser owns its own facilities and employs its own doctors. A patient must choose a Kaiser primary care doctor as their first point of contact—the gatekeeper—for referral to a specialist.

Corporate

In corporate medicine, physicians work as employees of a corporate management group. A few examples are One Health, TeamHealth, Mednax, Enserch, and US Anesthesia Partners. The group is run as a corporation with non-medical administrators making business decisions and contracting their services out to hospitals or health systems. Some have physicians serving as MBA administrators. Corporate directors usually manage multiple specialties across many hospitals. It is common for a physician of a certain specialty to manage another physician of a different specialty within the corporate setting. This model has the same benefits to the physician as the hospital or health system model: guaranteed benefits and salary. In some cities, corporate groups can dominate the medical industry by providing services to an entire hospital or health system. In the current landscape, there is major consolidation happening with corporations. With sweeping acquisitions and consolidations, the industry may see two or three multi-specialty medical conglomerates in the US.

Private Practice

This is probably the most common and recognizable physician practice model. Practitioners who fall under this model file a tax form 1099, are generally viewed as independent contractors, and can either be solo or part of a group practice. Solo practitioners take on the burden and risk of all administrative duties of running their business, including results of all the ups and downs of business cycles. If there is a problem with fraud, the business suffers. Conversely, if a group practice leaves the area then the business will naturally get all the referrals.

Group practices will have one physician as the managing physician who does all administrative duties, guides the practice, and provides the vision. This person represents the group in meetings with the hospitals, oversees managed care contracts, handles personnel hiring and firing, and deals with office staff. If it is a large enough group—with more than fifty physicians—they will have an administrator or Chief Executive Officer (CEO). Most of the smaller group practices—those with fewer than fifty physicians—will use consultants to fill this role. These group practices may offer partnership or some form of limited partnership to share in the profits and expenses.

I have made plenty of mistakes with my own practice. For example, hiring the wrong people and trusting the wrong advisors. But one of the smartest things I did prior to starting my own practice was negotiating an exclusive contract with the hospital to close the Level-2 nursery to the pediatricians. This is how I quickly learned about hospital politics. Remember the story about the pediatricians pulling out of the hospital in Houston due to a lawsuit that the jury ruled against the pediatrician? Well, my first day on the job, I was notified that there would be an emergency meeting of the pediatric department. *What an odd way to welcome me to the hospital*, I thought. I soon understood why they had called the meeting. At that meeting, I was greeted by the pediatricians all sitting across the table from me. They first welcomed me to the hospital and then proceeded to tell me how they expected things would work out. They wanted me to attend all high-risk deliveries, but turn over the care of the babies to them. They would consult me if needed.

There was a moment of silence as I digested this new development. I grabbed a piece of paper and asked each one of the pediatrician's to write down their contact information. The first two pediatricians wrote down their names and office information. But the third pediatrician had a question: "Why do you need all this information? After all, you haven't said a word about our demands."

Politely, I said, "I need your correct name and addresses so my attorney can send a certified letter about a potential breach of contract." That comment was met with gasps from the entire room. "You see, I have an exclusive contract with the hospital. Your demands are interfering with an executed and binding contract. That demonstrates breach." They quickly changed their minds and decided to give me a chance to develop the Level-2 nursery as stipulated in the contract.

Politics is all about power, control, and money. Once I understood this, I had to learn what the hospitals were looking for and how to speak their language so I could make myself invaluable to them. How did I do this? Most hospitals care about clinical excellence. But what do they care more about? Profit and losses. I was able to educate the CEO about the value of having a Level-2 or Level-3 nursery, a higher acuity nursery that could generate more money for the hospital if coding and billing were done correctly. This starts with the staff putting the correct daily charges and the

CFO having the right charges in the system. Every 24 hours, the charges are placed at midnight for the previous 24 hours. These must be captured correctly, or the hospital fails to benefit from the charge of higher acuity. This is what I had to show the hospital to make myself invaluable to them. And I got very good at this.

Over time, I was able to add more hospital contracts through word of mouth from the system chiefs. I got the right people in to help me build the practice, then I started my own billing company. I got a good accountant and a bank willing to extend me a line of credit. With a good corporate attorney to set up the PA and help with employment and hospital contracts. Eventually, I had built the company to fifteen hospital contracts over four different cities in Texas. The business continued to expand out of necessity because there is no safety in having just one hospital contract. Hospitals get bought out and administration changes all the time. Relationships I had cultivated could be gone in an instant. Plus, there's no loyalty among physicians.

Early in my career, I expanded the practice to a second hospital and built that nursery from a well-baby Level-1 nursery to a Level-2. This attracted the attention of the bigger systems in Houston. They wanted this contract. The obstetricians were all behind me and would speak up to support my group. But when the time came, not a single obstetrician stood up and opposed the decision by the hospital administration to change groups. After the meeting, they told me that they had to look after their own interests. This was a wake-up call for me that reinforced the fact that I couldn't rely on anyone. Because of this I kept expanding the number of contracts. Plus, this was my exit strategy. The more contracts in different geographical locations the more valuable the practice would be.

The result was that I was able to sell my practice for a large sum of money. The news quickly spread across the nation and was even mentioned on the CNBC ticker tape and in a press release. That day, I received a call from one of my brothers.

"Hey, I'm watching CNBC and saw your company flash across the screen," he said. "It says you've been acquired by a national company. Is that true?"

I could hear the shock and surprise in his voice. "Yes, it's true. That's me," I said.

Eventually, my dad called to congratulate me on the sale of my company. He had no idea that he had been the inspiration for me to not fail or give up. "I never thought you would wind up being the most successful of all my sons," he said with a chuckle.

I laughed too. Little did he know of the struggles and difficulties I had endured to reach this point in my life and career.

Academic Medicine

This is like practices run by a hospital or health system except it is focused more on an academic or teaching approach. The hospitals are usually part of a large, state-operated university system. Here, the physician's role is not just clinical, but also conducting research and teaching residents and medical students. Research can be clinical or bench research (basic science research), and physicians are required to publish their findings regularly in a peer-reviewed journal. There's a saying in academia: "Publish or perish." This is very true. The salary in academic medicine is often much lower than in private practice, but the benefits for employees and their families, as well as the retirement plans, are much more generous, which could outweigh the lower salary.

Locum Tenens

Sometimes, it may be beneficial to delay a permanent placement and go the route of a locum tenens, where you are temporary help. The term comes from the Latin phrase locum tenens, which means "to hold a place" or "to substitute for." There are quite a few locum companies out there. Some employers hire locums for long stretches—two weeks up to three months or more—until the permanent replacement gets their license or privileges. If your life circumstances cause you to seek a more flexible career move, consider a locum tenen position. A locum position has its advantages as well as its disadvantages. Some practices use locum tenens as a bridge before finding a permanent replacement. Locum positions give you the advantage of working at your convenience and, therefore, may be advantageous for new or retiring physicians, or for those in the midst of relocating to a new city or reconsidering their long- or short-term career objectives.

There are no employee benefits with this model, and physicians are paid a lump sum based on the rates of the locum tenens company. These locum tenens companies are the middleman and get a percentage or a commission from the employer—often a hospital group or a private practice—for their placement. Always ask what your fees will be prior to signing a contract. Locum companies will purchase your group malpractice insurance coverage, so be sure to confirm what the coverage amount is for malpractice.

From the employer's perspective, locums cost more. One important note to keep in mind is that employers have up to four weeks to cancel an assignment without penalties. So, a locum position might not be confirmed until four weeks prior to the assignment. In other words, it's not a guarantee until it's confirmed.

Look for the best position possible for you and your situation. No position is perfect. Sometimes, the position you apply for is a temporary stop for you in your career. If so, be truthful with the employer so they understand your intentions. Most employers are looking for permanent solutions and not temporary ones, but good employers will work out an arrangement with you if they consider you a good physician. Even a part-time or temporary position is better than no job at all.

After I sold my practice, I considered a locums position. I would get confirmed for an assignment and then get canceled four weeks before the start date. That was frustrating for me because had I not already committed to the position, I could have confirmed someplace else or made travel plans for the same time period. For that reason, locum didn't work for me. However, there are lots of people who work as locum and love it. My advice is to do locum toward the end of your career rather than at the beginning because it gives you the best time flexibility. When done early in your career, future employers will examine all those locum positions and wonder why you couldn't land a permanent position. Moonlighting would be an excellent temporary solution, but not a permanent one. For me, a moonlighter doesn't carry as much baggage as a locum tenen.

Graduate Studies

After graduation, researchers may elect to stay on and get a PhD. This allows you to further your academic career and solidify your position as an academic physician. Some graduates are highly sought after with this degree in academics especially when conducting bench or basic science research. Salary, benefits, and retirement are much the same as if you are still in training until you get the degree. The most likely employment route after graduate studies is academia.

Military

These are the health professional scholarship programs (HPSP) that offer two-, three-, and four-year scholarships that pay for tuition and related fees and provide a monthly stipend. There is also the Uniformed Services University of the Health Sciences (USU), which requires you to serve in the military to fill your obligations with different branches.

Finding job listings for any of the above options might seem like a monumental task, but it isn't. If there is a specific practice, hospital group, corporation, or university you have targeted as your ideal place to work, visit their website often to review job openings. You might also subscribe to trade publications and websites to view the latest job postings. Finally, recruiters will also post job opportunities on their websites.

Assessing Your Career Options

Choosing the best career option might seem daunting if you have several offers right out of medical school. Or it might seem like a no-brainer because you have one or two options, so you think going with the highest salary makes the most sense. Stop right there. Choosing the best option as you begin your career as a physician is one of the most important decisions you will make. Do not rush into it or be distracted by the lure of money. You want to make the best choice for yourself, your family, and your future. Understanding what you are getting into with your employer gives you the upper hand on day one and allows you to chart a career path that keeps your best interest front and center. Remember, medicine is a business, and you must treat it as such. Do your due diligence with every offer you have. This takes time, so don't rush into it or be pressured to give them an answer right away.

Here are some things to consider as you review each of your employment options:

Their reputation. Learn how the practice, office, or hospital works. What are the departments? Where do you fit in? What are their ratings or reviews? You could visit Yelp or Google for reviews, but these sites typically include complaints from patients about their bills or those airing their grievances, which isn't necessarily helpful to you. In contrast, HealthGrades.com can provide more useful reviews and information for your employment purposes. Other sites to look at are Hospitalsafetygrade.org, leapfroggroup.org, usnews.com, and webmd.com. There are also many sites to check a physician's reputation. These include HealthGrades.com, RateMDs.com, Zocdoc.com, and rater8.com. Also, research their history of malpractice and other complaints by visiting the national databank for malpractice—also known as the National Practitioner Data Bank (NPDB)—or state website disciplinary section. I routinely do this for potential new physician hires.

Their culture. This encompasses a lot of factors that impact your work/life balance and enjoyment of your work, including how the practice or group views family priorities, the value they place on a physician's mental health, administrative support and the lack of bureaucracy, collaboration among physicians and staff, reputation (as noted above), and more. So, how do you learn about the culture of a practice or group? Consider a bit of guerrilla research. You'd be surprised to know what you can learn simply by talking to the owner of the donut shop next door to the practice, the folks in the HR or IT departments, the nurses, or the billing staffers. To access a resource with a list of questions that can provide insights into the culture of a practice or medical group, visit thebusinessofmedicine. net/bookresources.

Company culture includes:

- how employees communicate with each other
- how decisions are made
- how people are hired
- how employees are recognized
- how employees celebrate their work and each other

As an employer, I also observe whether you are a good fit culturally for the staff and physicians already employed. These are some of the questions I would ask you to see if you would fit into our group. Think about these questions and your responses.

- Describe your ideal work environment for me.
- What gets you excited about coming to work?
- What did you like most/least about the last company you worked for?
- How could a manager best support you?

- How do you handle stress or difficult patients?
- What favorite websites or podcasts do you follow?
- What motivates you to do your best work?
- How do you prefer to communicate with coworkers?
- What would your ideal work schedule look like?
- Would you rather work alone or in a team?

Their competition. I think it's fair to ask about a group's competitor. As an employer, I knew everything about my competition—their culture, the way they operated, how they did their billing and collections, how they were structured, and who was in charge administratively. As a future hire, ask the following questions of your potential employer. If they don't know the answers off the top of their heads, or if they find this line of questioning off-putting, then this is not the practice for you.

- Who is your main competitor?
- What makes your practice different from your competition?
- Why should a patient choose your practice over a competitor?
- How do you plan to stay ahead of the competition?
- Where do you see this practice in the next five years?

Their offer. As an employer, the offer is something I usually do not like to talk about during the interview process. Should you ask me about the offer during the interview, it will immediately have a negative impact on me. But that's me personally. Offers depend on your years of experience. New grads are usually offered entry-level salary; that's just standard. Other salary considerations include: your board certification (better to be boarded than not), and the location of the job (rural areas will command a higher salary compared to bigger cities). Don't expect a lateral move with salary if you are moving from a rural area back to a bigger city.

I once had a doctor apply for work in my practice who had been working in a small, rural town earning over $500,000 a year. He wanted to make a lateral move to Houston and expected equal compensation. He had a hard time understanding why I couldn't pay him that amount in Houston. I had to explain to him that he deserved that pay at his current employer because he was the only one on the job. Matching that salary just wasn't possible in the larger metropolitan area because there was such a bigger pool of physician talent to choose from. My final advice for him was to get his school loans paid off and get a good financial advisor.

You can certainly ask about eligibility for partnership, but be prepared for this discussion. You will need to know how and when partnership is possible. Usually there is a road map for this. Don't expect to take a copy of the partnership paperwork home. Instead, wait on their offer letter and then ask more questions later. That's when the real negotiation begins.

Your goals. Review the goals exercise in the previous chapter. Be sure the offer fits with your defined goals. There is no skirting around this. Do not expect for a gloomy opportunity to suddenly become a ray of sunshine. If it looks bad at the start it will likely remain that way or get worse, so don't go into it with rose-colored glasses. This is your future. Make sure the offer fits with your goals. If working yourself out of your student loans is a goal, consider the benefit of this to the employer and the long-term impact on your earnings. This kind of offer is typically found in rural areas and comes with high pay. The military or government also will offer to pay off student loans, but you have to commit to a number of years to fulfill your obligations. The problem is that you can't market yourself at the same rates elsewhere.

One other important consideration is to cut your losses early. If, once you are hired, you find that any aspect of your new job is less fulfilling than you thought it would be, or if your employer has suddenly withdrawn parts of their written offer, give it a chance, but also set a deadline for your exit; maybe a year or two. Remember that your experience at this job will be added to your resumé. Your next employer will ask why you left your previous job.

Your family. As stated in the previous chapter, if you are married, engaged, have children, or are otherwise responsible for or concerned with other family members, you must consult with them on your career opportunities. What you choose as your first or next job in medicine will impact them at some point. Be sure they understand everything you have learned about the offers you receive. Family can act as a support system. They can give you a different perspective on the job offer and how it will impact your family life.

Do not succumb to the pressure of a tight timeline to submit your response to an offer. You deserve time to consider an offer. Any practice or hospital that requires you to respond in less than 72 hours is suspect. You must ask yourself why they are so rushed. In most cases, this will not be the best fit for you because they are likely hiring out of some level of desperation: either a physician recently quit or was let go (find out why); they have to fill a quota to receive funding or other benefits (learn more); the environment is toxic (see above under culture); or some other reason. Just be aware and be cautious.

Finally, never appear desperate and in need of work. People can smell that. Don't beg for a job. This will get you the worst possible offer and leave you regretting your decision within a very short time. If you have been on several interviews over months and have not found a good fit for you, don't despair. You must believe that the right job is available for you in the right location, the right setting, and with the right salary. Remember, the world needs great physicians, and the right opportunity could be just around the corner.

Interview Skills

By the time you get the invitation to interview for your first job as a physician, you will probably have been on other interviews in your life. The same basic interview skills apply to you as a physician candidate. Preparation, personality, and punctuality are three keys to start the interview off on the right foot. Let's explore each in detail:

- **Preparation.** Learn about the practice, their specialization, the boss, and key partners. Also, be prepared to ask some questions about the practice or group. Of course, the interviewer will ask you several questions, but you should be armed with questions of your own. There should be a free flow of information between you and your potential employer.

- **Personality.** Personal appearance is extremely important. Just as you might judge a book by its cover, your interviewer will judge you by the way you look. That's just the way it is. Help make your first impression a positive one. Dress professionally, even for virtual interviews. This includes a slightly conservative wardrobe that includes clothing that is clean and pressed. Get a haircut and style your hair. Shave. Take the interview seriously. Regarding your conversation and demeanor, don't be too relaxed or laid back, but try to be as comfortable as possible. Be authentic when sharing information about yourself, but don't over-share by offering unrelated or irrelevant information. Act interested and not bored or detached. Listen earnestly to information shared and ask questions related to the practice or group, the staff, patients, and overall working culture. For a list of questions you could ask during an interview, visit thebusinessofmedicine.net/bookresources.

- **Punctuality.** Be respectful of the interviewer's time by showing up on time. Be early. Even if you show up early and have to wait for them, that is better than them having to wait for you to arrive. Besides, by showing up early you have a chance to get a feel for the office environment, which could put you at ease. I once had an interviewee show up thirty minutes late and they had no good excuse for their tardiness. That was a negative flag against them. Don't cause this to happen to you.

Typically, the first interview is held virtually via a video platform or by phone. This allows the interviewer to get to know you and determine if you have the personality to fit the corporate culture before inviting you in for a more formal interview. Remember, that first impression is extremely important in determining whether the employer takes the next step with you.

If you make it to round two, the follow-up interview will be held in person at the practice location. The practice will pay for all expenses to get you to their location, including air fare or ground transportation costs and accommodations. For in-person interviews that take place out of town for you, plan to be there for at least a full day. In some instances, two days might be required, depending on how many representatives you interview with, how long the interviews last, and how far you need to travel to return home. The practice will have an itinerary for when you arrive, which often includes meeting other physicians in the practice, as well as administrators, and even someone from human resources to review benefits options.

Before you sign on the dotted line, you will want to find out learn more about the culture of the practice (as mentioned previously), learn how physicians engage with the administration at a hospital, and behaviors that are forbidden among staffers. You also want to know about the short- and long-term plans for the practice and its ownership. Find out where the practice is heading in the next three to five years. Additionally, ask to view their strategic plan and growth plan. Find out if there are plans for expansion or sale of the practice and if there is an exit plan for the partners and physicians. Although they may be surprised you've asked these pointed questions, the interviewer should have clear and specific answers to each of these questions. Also, ask them where they see you within the practice in three to five years. Be sure you are able to answer this question as well. Finally, ask about benefits. Does the practice provide term life insurance, malpractice insurance (and what kind), paid time off (PTO), vacation time, and spousal benefits?

Understanding the needs, expectations, and concerns of the other side of the table—your potential employer—is helpful in building rapport and a healthy respect for your potential employer. Employers are not merely looking for any physician to fill a slot; they are seeking exceptional clinicians who can operate within and enhance a stable work environment. They want to avoid high turnover, lawsuits for malpractice, discrimination, and sexual harassment. So, choosing the right person for the job is critical for them.

Be Prepared to Answer These Questions

After twenty-seven years of practicing medicine, growing my knowledge, and gaining some savvy about the business of medicine, I moved to the other side of the table. As founder of my own private practice, I was responsible for screening and hiring new physicians. That experience showed me how easy it is to take advantage of new, unsuspecting, naive graduates who didn't know what I knew. Of course, I never took advantage of any new hires, but I did learn how ill-prepared they were for not only their new job, but also for the interview itself.

In any interview, there are some common questions you will get. None of them are "trick" questions, per se, but they are designed to give the interviewer some insight into your personality and how you think, make decisions, communicate, and formulate appropriate responses.

Never negotiate during the interview process.

During my first interview out of med school, I was extremely nervous and probably did everything wrong. Heck, I didn't know anything, nor did I have a mentor. When I became chief resident, I interviewed many potential pediatric interns and got a lot more experience with the interview process. Today, thirty years later, the landscape is even more competitive, and interviewers have more psychological background to assess potential physicians. Your best weapon for success is to go into an interview thinking from the employer's perspective.

Open-ended questions are very common in interviews. They are designed to get you talking, to gauge how you think and communicate your thoughts, and to measure how comfortable you are speaking on a specific topic. A simple approach to answering open-ended questions is to first provide a straightforward reply, then follow up with a brief story about yourself or an experience you had. Be sure your response is truthful and relevant to the question. Avoid rambling. Once you have answered the question and shared your brief story, stop talking.

Here are some common questions you might receive during an interview, and even a few you hope you don't get:

- **Tell me about yourself.** The interviewer wants to know something about you that is not on your resumé. The fact that they called you in for the interview suggests that they already know about your academic and clinical experience, so refrain from regurgitating your medical qualifications. Instead, share a positive personal story about yourself or mention a characteristic you feel will help you in the position.

- **What are your strengths?** Mention a few strengths that best match what you can bring to the table. Talk about things in your life that you had to overcome. Don't embellish, brag, or make yourself out to be a hero. I once had a candidate mention that his certification in the neonatal resuscitation program

(NRP) is why he deserved a salary commensurate with mine. In fact, that certification was a requirement for the job; it was not a strength.

- **What are your weaknesses?** This is not an open door to be self-deprecating. Instead, mention one or two personal characteristics you are working to improve that are not important to the role you're applying for. State your answer in a way that suggests you are taking measures to correct those deficits. For example: "I would like to enhance my ability to speak Spanish fluidly and I'm using a language app to help so I can better communicate with Spanish-speaking patients and their families."

- **What's your ideal job?** Be careful with your answer. No job will be perfect. Don't come across as living in a dreamland. As an employer, I want to see if your expectation is realistic or not. Think carefully before answering this question. Consider including in your response some characteristics of the ideal work environment for you, the types of people you most enjoy working with, the pace at which you generally perform best. State that you are flexible with all of this, but that this is your ideal.

- **What interests you about this position?** As mentioned earlier, be prepared by researching the practice beforehand, especially the mission and culture, in addition to the role you are applying for. Be honest and show some interest in the position. Perhaps you heard great things about the practice from a colleague, or you learned that they have an annual giving campaign that has made a positive impact on the local community, or you appreciate that they practice sustainable efforts to lower their carbon footprint, or they have been awarded a "Best places to work" recognition. Maybe this position will allow you to further enhance your interest and experience in a specific area. Again, be sure to reference actual points that are true.

- **What made you decide to become a (whatever specialty)?** Answer truthfully. Foreign medical graduates, please tell me why you chose neonatology if you were a surgeon in your home country. Employers want to know your motivation and passion for your specialty. If you have a personal story to tie to this, share it. If your mother was an OB and wanted you to follow in her footsteps, share that.

- **Have you taken the boards yet?** I have had candidates try to hide that they've taken the boards several times and failed them. If this is the case, be truthful and have an explanation, but don't lie. Tell them what you're doing to try to pass the boards. Board certification is extremely important for insurance plans, so you need to stay on top of board eligibility requirements. All hospitals require board certification within a certain time frame. Don't ignore these requirements.

- **Do you have any malpractice claims currently or pending against you?** In my private practice, I once asked a doctor if he had any suits against him. He answered that he had no claims. When I looked at the national data bank there were four cases pending against him. This made me suspicious of him immediately. Don't try to be coy. Being honest with your answer is much better than having the employer find out later. Now, I ask if there are any malpractice claims currently or pending.

- **Why did you leave your previous job?** Be honest. Odds are that the employer will check references. If they're like me, they won't call the references provided in your resumé but will instead call the program director or other physicians they know at your previous job because they will provide an honest answer. This is why it is especially important to never burn any of your bridges. Don't trash the office on the way out or create a scandal and then leave. Never bad mouth your former boss. People tend to remember these things. Plus, karma is a bitch.

- **What are the goals you have set for yourself for the next five years?** Prior to showing up at your interview, you should seriously consider what you are looking for in your first or next place of employment. Where do you see yourself in the next five, ten, or fifteen years? Here is your opportunity to show that you have thought about achievable goals related to your career and life. Don't say you want to be the next Dr. Giep. Flattery won't get you where you need to be. Instead, mention a stretch goal that suggests you have high expectations for your career, but not something outlandish. For example, you might wish to be a shareholder in the future. Share how you plan to achieve this goal.

- **How have you handled adversity in your career or life?** Talk about your communication skills while being a leader. How did you deal with a difficult family or patient? If you have personal stories, tell them. This is not the time to be a downer. The point of this question is for you to demonstrate what you learned and how you successfully solved a problem in your life. Above all, avoid talking bad about any of your colleagues or previous employer.

- **What do you like to do in your time off?** Here, the interviewer wants to know about your life outside of medicine. What makes you tick? What are your hobbies? Do you have any interests besides medicine? As stated earlier, don't be boring. Be prepared to share one or two hobbies or areas of interest where you are expanding your knowledge. For me, it is cooking and traveling.

- **Do you have any questions for me?** You're almost guaranteed to be asked this question. Be prepared. Never say no to this one. Show that you have been listening and have researched the company. Ask HR-type questions, such as, how they handle patient complaints or harassment in the office. Don't ask about moonlighting or pay raises as this could be a red flag for employers. You can ask these questions one you get an offer letter and contract.

- **Is there anything we didn't get to discuss?** You will be tempted to say no, but don't. This is another opportunity to communicate specific areas of interest or concern to the interviewer. You might ask how they would define the corporate culture, what they wished they had known about the practice before starting there, or what advice they would give a new physician on day one. Ask if the practice is part of a local practice, group practice, hospital-owned group, private practice, for-profit organization, or not-for-profit organization. Don't bring up subjects that may be too sensitive, such as you heard that there's a pending litigation. End by asking about the process to decide on the best candidate for the position, what the next step is, who will contact you, and who you might contact with questions related to the employment contract.

The point behind these questions is to see how well-balanced you are and how well you communicate. Essentially, employers want to make sure you're not a walking psychopath.

As you sit across from your new employer's HR director, you might get the sense that you can negotiate everything in your contract. You're wrong. Never negotiate during the interview process. Negotiation happens only after you have received an offer letter or letter of intent and then you will get a formal contract. The contract is in place to protect the employer and to ensure you abide by their rules of engagement. It does not exist to satisfy your need for security. In a later chapter we discuss that there are very few areas of an employment contract that are negotiable, which is why you are advised to hire a healthcare attorney. Let your attorney do the negotiation.

Beware of Red Flags

When you enter an interview prepared and confident, with your eyes wide open, you are equipped to spot red flags that might pop up in the interview. Red flags are warnings for you to be aware of regarding the culture, integrity, and accepted behaviors of the potential workplace. Pay attention to everything in the interview from the moment you enter the office. This includes the cleanliness of the facility, the attitudes of the staff you encounter, how long you wait to be called in by the interviewer, how prepared they are for you, and their demeanor during the interview. All these experiences provide insight into the employer's work environment.

To be even more specific, be aware of the following red flags during your interviews:

Predators: Although this might sound dramatic, believe me when I tell you that predators in the business of medicine do exist. Some practices will hire new graduates and then not renew their contract after three years. This is to keep the overhead cost low. As you will read in the next chapter, negotiating annual increases in your compensation is common. That is a great benefit for the physician, but it costs the practice in the long run. Why pay more for an experienced physician when they could pay a new graduate a lower starting salary? With this kind of behavior, predators create a revolving door for new physicians. This is quite prevalent in rural clinics, where physicians with visa requirements or a weak CV are easily taken advantage of. To help avoid this, find out the length of time each of the current physicians has been on staff at the practice. If none have been there longer than three years, consider that a red flag.

Workload: Ask about the patient volume. Will there be any backup should you get overwhelmed? Will the office manager add patients in between scheduled patients without prior notice to you? Some practices are so understaffed that the workload becomes unbearable. This will lead to burnout and a possible early exit.

Bait and Switch: If the job discussed during the interview sounds different from the initial job description, this is to get you in the door and convince you that this position is a good fit for you. Don't fall for this trick. The initial job description needs to be clear and concise.

Desperation: If they seem desperate to find someone to fill a position, ask yourself why. An urgency to hire you, without a fair amount of time to consider their offer, is a red flag. A hurried hiring process on their part is a red flag. Mentally divide the interview process into before, during, and after the interview. Each aspect should be given a fair amount of time for both you and the employer to consider and decide.

Here are some red flags to watch for at each stage:
Before the interview:

- Unclear or inefficient scheduling of the interview is indicative of how the organization operates.
- Incorrect information about where to go and who you are interviewing with indicates poor communication.
- A job description that is unclear speaks volumes about the organization's lack of clarity for its overall vision.
- Too many people involved in the pre-interview process often indicates disorganization. Think of this like calling customer service and being transferred from one department to another only to get hung up on before you resolve your issue.

During the interview:

- How they treat employees is a direct reflection on the leaders.
- Conflicting values suggests that all decisions must be run by a partner first, which could be a problem for you down the road.
- The interviewer asking highly inappropriate or even illegal questions.
- How the organization deals with change. Does everything have to be approved by the head physician? What if he doesn't approve? Is it his way or the highway?
- The absence of an organizational chart may be indicative of disorganization. How are decisions made? Who has the final say?

After the interview:

- No follow up. You wait and wait, and no there is further communication. This is especially important if during the interview you asked when the decision would be made about the position and that time has come and gone with no word from the practice. By the way, be sure to send a thank-you letter following the interview.
- Long delays with the letter of intent. Sometimes things are busy, but if two weeks have passed before you receive a letter of intent, this may indicate that legal or HR is overworked. Impressions are everything.
- Even longer delays in formal employment contracts. There should be a sample standard employment contract in every HR office. There is no excuse for long delays after negotiations are completed. It is not uncommon to wait for a revised contract after all negotiations are complete and all terms are agreed upon.

- Mistakes in the employment contract. This should not be happening. Serious red flag.

As a new physician interviewing for a new job, you should objectively look for these red flags. Doing so could save you a lot of heartache in the short term. Ask questions to clarify any perceived disorganization or expected communication. Address any red flags to help clear the air so that there is no misunderstanding about any aspect of the new position. After all, you are vetting them as much as they are vetting you.

When I interviewed for my job in Savannah, I observed everyone being very nervous around the principal shareholder. It was clear that she was in charge. I thought it was a sign of respect. But shortly after coming on board, I realized that it was more like fear. She ruled with an iron fist, and everything had to be done her way or else. If I had known then what I know now, I would have counted that early experience as a red flag.

Trust your gut when it comes to these and other red flags in interviews. Even if it means passing on what seems like a great opportunity, you will likely thank yourself later.

VETTING A PRACTICE AND ITS REPUTATION

What keeps physicians around? Reputation, ownership/ governance model, compensation, and benefits. These issues are critical for you when considering a practice, hospital, or medical group as your place of employment. The reason it is important for you to know and understand the reputation of any practice you are considering is the same reason they want to know about your reputation: one reflects the other. During the interview, they will tell you all the best things about the practice, but there is always more to the story than what they let on. Once you say yes to a job offer, you are now considered part of that practice's ecosystem and reputation. So, you might as well know what you're getting into before signing a contract.

Compare the process of vetting the practice to that of buying a car. You research the brand and its rating on *Car and Driver* magazine, but you still want to look under the hood and take it for a spin.

How do you go about learning the reputation of a practice before you are hired? You need to do your homework. The first place to look is their website. They should have one. If they don't, you have your answer. Their website will have an "About" section showing who the founders are and explaining the origins, mission, and vision of the practice. There should also be a section titled "Meet Our Team" or something similar. A list of the doctors and nurse practitioners or physician's assistants with their educational background should be available. A section on frequently asked questions is also common. Read through this information carefully as it provides insight into who is in charge and how the practice operates, essentially a peek into their workplace culture.

Many of the more advanced practices will have a portal to schedule appointments, handle paying bills, and even leave text messages for the provider. This indicates some level of adoption of technology and automation, which shows some use of modern systems. In the 21st century, this is important as many administrative functions require technology. You don't want to be stuck working at a practice that is averse to innovation and technological advancements.

When you are ready to dig a little deeper into the way the practice and its staff are perceived by outsiders, you'll have to roll up your sleeves and do a little guerrilla research. Sometimes, when I'm evaluating a hospital, I visit a nearby diner or coffee shop and talk to the waitress or server. They have seen patients and staff come and go from the facility, have overheard conversations (maybe gossip) from their patrons, and witnessed some good and bad behaviors that you might want to be aware of. I once had a waitress tell me when I asked about the hospital, "I wouldn't take my dog there," implying that patients go there at their own peril. Waitresses are typically more than happy to give you the scoop on a facility. Ask them, "Would you take a family member to this hospital's labor and delivery or emergency room?" "Does this practice support any local groups or charities in the community?" "Have you ever noticed any drama between patients and staff?" Granted, all of this is hearsay, but it could be insightful as you make your decision whether to work there.

In addition to talking to outsiders, be sure to initiate casual conversations with those within the hospital or practice. Most doctors at the practice can say only so much because they are held to a non-disclosure agreement (NDA). However, nurses aren't under an NDA. Ask nurses, administrators, lab technicians, and other staff about their experiences at the practice. They will know about the frequency of physician turnover, how well the organizational structure works, patient outcomes (good and bad), the impact of malpractice suits on day-to-day operations, and the overall culture of the practice or hospital group. Take the staff's insights to heart because they live it every day.

Here are some other considerations to keep in mind as you vet a practice:

Physician turnover. During the interview, find out as much information as possible about the turnover rate. High turnover is a bad sign. A practice or department that gets a new staff every year is considered a very high turnover rate. Some practices are a revolving door for physicians, mostly for financial reasons because hiring a new physician is much cheaper than keeping one with experience. Calling former doctors regarding their experience at the practice may offer a mixed bag of information—some reliable, some not. I found out during my early career, that a practice may put a gag clause in their employment contract for physicians as a condition of termination. Usually, the employee is asked to sign a non-disclosure agreement or release from liabilities agreement.

Vision for the practice. Do the practice members have a clear vision for the practice over the next five years? Do they differ from one another? Do they have a culture? What is the culture? Do they have confidence in the leadership? Are they clear with the mission statement? What is their mission statement? Are they expanding their practice? Are the senior partners about to retire? Maybe they're going to sell the practice during your tenure. You want to consider how that will impact your career. Ask for reassurance in how they deal with the many changes in healthcare. Does clinical management differ from provider to provider? How does the provider handle different clinical management? Do the orders change completely when a new provider takes over? Ask these questions during the interview.

Geographic location. You may want to be located in a certain region or city due to obligations to your family or spouse. When choosing your geographic location, make sure your spouse agrees with the location. My wife would never want to move to a small town. She's a big-city person and likes concrete buildings. Remember, "Happy wife, happy life!" Generally, relocating to a larger metropolitan area comes with lower pay and more benefits. This is due primarily to the fact that the employer assumes the lure of big-city life—with an array of entertainment options, school choices for kids, and a more well-rounded social life—are all benefits in and of themselves. If you decide to go with a lucrative contract in a small town, you might have more opportunities to negotiate things like your employer paying off your student loan. Pay attention to payer mix in these small towns. They are usually high with Medicare/Medicaid patients. This is why the salary is guaranteed and much higher. The hospitals are most likely getting a high disproportional care distribution from the government.

Organizational Structure

Requesting a copy of the medical group's organizational chart is a must, particularly for a big organization. Bigger organizations have a clear structure with a CEO, CFO, COO, CMO, CNO, and maybe even a CQO: the C-suite people as I call it. They may be physicians with or without an MBA, or they could be hospital administrators.

Talk to them and find out what their role is, how long they have been in their position, and what their vision is for the group. For a smaller, office-based practice, the hierarchy should be quite clear and, therefore, the org chart might not be necessary.

For any practice or medical group, you want to know who makes the decisions and how decisions are made. The org chart will show you how many partners are in the group and which administrative roles report to each partner. This will give you a better understanding of how responsibilities are handled and how decisions flow through the organization. Become familiar with the organizational structure before you accept a position. Whether you plan to use your time at the practice as a bridge to another, more lucrative or visible position elsewhere, or you plan to remain at the practice and become a partner, you should understand the structure and nuances of the practice.

To Partner or Not

Have you considered partnership as a career goal? Many new physicians have aspirations of one day earning partnership in a group or practice. Be an owner. This is certainly a worthy career goal, but becoming partner is not for everyone. Learn everything you can about the roles and responsibilities of a partner. When you do, you might find that it isn't all it's cracked up to be or that it's just not for you. In your role as an employee, your responsibility is limited to patient care and reporting to your group manager. Therefore, you bear none of the financial responsibility or administrative duties of the group. Sometimes, being a partner is not ideal. So, assess your position regularly over your employment at the practice. This will help you decide whether you want to pursue a partnership.

Partnership comes with many responsibilities, some of which might not be to your liking. If becoming partner is a goal of yours, there are some serious questions you should ask your potential employer before accepting an offer:

- Is partnership offered?
- How does one become a partner?
- What is the buy-in?
- What are the responsibilities of a partner?
- How long do you have to work before partnership is considered?
- Is the group financially stable?
- What are their long-term goals for growth?

You may not want to be a partner if the terms are not clear or don't align with your goals, so gather as much information as you can and determine early on if partnership is something you are interested in. Reassess your outlook on partnership often as you uncover more realities of working with the practice.

If you determine that partnership is something you want to go after, be aware of some of the intricacies that will impact your career. There is a reason that earning partnership takes years. This is a decision you and the practice do not enter into lightly. For your role, don't become a partner with an employee vision. I've encountered these types of partners who only want profits and dividends. They're not participating in the growth of the practice. They think that performing their clinical responsibilities is all they need to do. Being a partner in a medical practice requires much more than that. Once you make it to the ranks of partner, your outlook on the business of medicine should be completely different than it was when you started at the practice as a physician. You should have learned some insights into the practice, how it's run, who the key players are, and what their long-term vision is.

Groups routinely add partners to dilute their financial share of the overhead. Typically, there is a buy-in amount to become a partner to ensure each partner has some skin in the game and ownership. Sharing overhead with an increasing number of shareholders reduces overhead for each partner. Profit sharing is the earning side of a partnership, where each partner receives a portion of the profits earned by the practice. The process, formula, or calculations for profit sharing should be clearly structured and explained. The other side of the profit/loss equation is the losses. Partners do not get to benefit from the earnings and avoid the hit when there are losses. I have seen plenty of examples in my career where partners are only interested in profits, but don't take on the burden when there is a loss. Some practices also own interests in ancillary businesses, such as real estate properties, after -hours clinics, aesthetic clinics, sleep labs, or urgent care clinics. Each of these factor into the profit/loss equation of a partnership.

Another often unspoken aspect of a partnership is buy-outs. Ask the group if they are in discussion to be bought out by another group. They may not tell you upfront, but if they hesitate then you know the answer. Because of the intricacies involved in becoming a partner of a medical practice, you would be wise to hire a medical consultant and a corporate attorney to help you navigate whether you want to be a partner.

Early in my career I had an offer to join a group. I asked about partnership and was told that I would have to be an employee for at least three years before being considered for partnership. There were no guarantees after three years. I suspected that they just wanted to eliminate competition. I turned down the opportunity. Three months later, they announce their sale to a big national group. Obviously, they had been in discussion with them for a while. Had I accepted the offer, the future of my career would have been impacted by the buy-out.

Sweat equity has also come up in my career. This is when you work for a set number of years and automatically become a partner due to the investment of time you have invested. I wholeheartedly dislike this idea. Merely putting up three years of work shouldn't automatically gain you a seat at the table. Hard work alone doesn't earn you the right or privilege of partnership, nor does it prove you deserve it or have earned the titled of partner.

Compensation Package

The compensation package should be clearly defined in an offer letter and then in a contract. Sometimes, a sign-on bonus is included. Don't expect this bonus to be awarded the moment you sign on the dotted line. Employers want you to sign and stay a while before giving you the bonus. In my practice, sign-on bonuses were awarded eighteen months after the start of employment. The contract should also include your starting salary and indicate that your salary will increase annually. The amount of increase is something you can negotiate. You might also negotiate a bonus for passing your boards. This is not usually offered, but it doesn't hurt to ask. Additionally, the contract should clearly state how much time you are expected to be on the job. If you are being hired to take on an additional role, then you should be compensated for it. For example, if you are to be the medical director over the sleep lab on top of being a staff physician in the practice, then you should be compensated for the title and the work.

Anything extra and beyond the scope of work for your physician role should be compensated in addition to your regular salary. For example, moonlighting with the group should be compensated. The MGMA website shows compensation for different specialties in different regions. There is a difference in pay from the East Coast compared to the West Coast. Similarly, don't expect the high pay in a rural area, where you might be the only doctor in town, to be comparable to that in an urban area, where there is a larger supply of talented physicians.

Another common compensation model is Relative Value Unit (RVU)-based compensation. This model is very common among practices. "Under the RVU compensation model, doctors are paid more for more complex procedures and services and earn a premium for working with patients requiring complicated medical care," says

Eric Rosenberg in a 2022 article in White Coat Investor.[3] He adds that RVUs are paid in three traunches: work RVU, practice expense RVU, and malpractice RVU. "Work RVUs make up about 45% and malpractice makes up roughly 5%. Practice expense is intended to cover the costs of labor and other operating expenses for the practice, including medical supplies, rent, and equipment." Once you add up your total RVU for a period, you can multiply that by the approved conversion factor. "Remember that geography is a factor in total RVUs earned, so you would earn more for a procedure in a high-cost area than in a low-cost area despite the same payment per RVU." Most physicians are employed by large health systems or hospital groups and RVU-based structures are common.

According to a 2022 study on physician compensation by Jackson Physician Search, these are the pros and cons of the RVU model.[4]

Pros

- The salary guarantee offers stability for new physicians and alleviates the pressure to ramp up in an unreasonable amount of time. As a new physician, this is what you want in your first employment contract.

- Productivity-based compensation gives physicians more income. The harder they work, the more income they will receive. Once you are established, this could work if you know that the practice can support this model.

- RVU compensation is typically not impacted by how much or how little the organization is able to collect from patients or their insurance companies. The payer mix also does not

---

[3] Eric Rosenberg, "RVU-Based Physician Compensation," The Write Coat Investor, November 16, 2022, https://www.whitecoatinvestor.com/rvu-compensation-models-for-physicians/
[4] "Physician Compensation 101: What Residency Didn't Teach You," Jackson Physician Search, April 4, 2022 (Updated August 29, 2024), https://www.jacksonphysiciansearch.com/insights/physician-compensation-models-what-residency-didnt-teach-you/

impact the physician's income, but the volume and acuity of the patients does.

Cons

- RVUs do not account for time spent on administrative work, meetings, mentoring other physicians, and other tasks without a CPT code. It is not an incentive for you to learn the business side of things.
- RVU-based compensation can create a culture of competition that prevents physicians from collaborating and supporting each other. In other words, you are a slave to your job.
- Productivity-based physician compensation puts a physician's focus on the quantity of procedures rather than the quality of care. The higher the acuity or complicated case the more procedures you will end up doing and the less patient volume you will experience.

When considering the RVU model, here are a few questions to ask.

- Is the physician salary guarantee a minimum base or is it also a cap? It is common to see an 80% salary minimum base and then the rest as RVU incentive or productivity pay.
- How many work RVUs do most physicians in this practice produce? You may not get this answer during the interview process, but you can ask.
- How does the productivity of physicians here compare to national norms?
- Is there a cap on RVU bonuses?

Private practice compensation models are different. They are usually initial salary with possible track to partnership. Efficiency of the practice has a direct impact on how much the partners earn.

Pros

- Physicians in private practice have a clearer view of the factors contributing to their income, that is, the revenue and expenses of the practice. They are also keener to changing markets and demographics.

- Employed physicians are limited to the hospital's bonus structure, but as a practice owner, you have unlimited income potential, as well as the potential to lose income. The risk is yours.

Cons

- Research shows that Medicare reimburses physician services billed by hospitals at a higher rate than those billed by independent practices. This is one of many reasons hospitals can afford to pay higher salaries.

- Because Medicare reimburses at a lower rate than private insurers, the practice's patient mix will impact its profits, and thus, partner income.

- Practicing medicine is already a stressful job. Physician partners in private practice have the added stress of taking on the risk of a business.

As noted, physician compensation will be tied to how well the practice performs, so ask enough questions to gain a full understanding. When considering various private practice options, here are a few questions to ask.

How busy is the practice? What is the patient mix?

How effective is the billing department in collecting payment? Is the billing department in-house or is it outsourced?

What are the overhead costs?

What can I expect to earn as a partner? Are there any opportunities for ancillary income, such as investing in an outpatient surgery center, real estate, or imaging? Is there a "buy-in" cost associated with becoming a partner or associated with those ancillary businesses?

Do all physician owners hold equal shares in the business? What about shares in the ancillary business?

Is there an accelerated track to partnership?

Are the partners currently considering selling to a hospital or corporate entity? What happens to a partner's shares if they retire or leave the practice?

Beyond Just the Money

A few other areas to consider when vetting a practice—particularly if you have more than one offer to consider—will help you make a decision that is best for you and your family. These include:

- Relocation Package
- Benefit Package
- Insurance
- Mentorship
- Patient Outcomes
- Culture

Relocation Package

A relocation package is commonly included in any offer letter. This includes moving allowances up to a certain dollar amount to cover transportation for you and your household goods. This amount can be paid either directly to the moving company or reimbursed to you after you present receipts. If your actual relocation expenses are less than the amount of the allowance, you are not permitted to pocket the difference. Do not ask the employer for this. It makes you look bad in their eyes. Some bigger organizations will offer a more robust relocation package. Buying your old house is out of the question, but if they really want you then you can negotiate other terms, such as the first three to four months lease for a new place, or travel expenses until your old house sells. Negotiate in advance what expenses you can get reimbursed for. All expenses will need a receipt; without one you will receive no refund. If your employer doesn't reimburse you, then use the receipts to deduct expenses on your federal income tax. Your employer will report everything to the IRS including the sign-on bonus.

Benefit Package

The benefit package is probably the most important besides the salary compensation. In general, state employees have better benefits packages than do for-profit organizations. Most employers will have a comprehensive benefit package. This will include health, disability, dental, vision, malpractice, life insurance, and 401k. Some employers offer a health savings account. Most of these insurances are not portable, meaning you cannot take them to your next employment. What you can take with you to your next place of employment is supplemental insurance offered by an employer. These include additional coverage, such as those offered by AFLAC. These plans cover everything from cancer treatments, critical care, accidents, final expense insurances, and supplemental income for hospitalization. Take advantage of these supplemental plans.

Additionally, your 401k plan is portable from one employer to the next, meaning you can take those funds with you when you leave. But don't act too quickly! Never accept a check or a transfer in the amount of your 401k into your personal checking or savings account as this will qualify as taxable income. Instead, upon leaving your current employer, you must roll over your 401k funds into either an IRA or a Roth IRA plan through your financial institution upon departure. You own the contributions you make to your 401k and any earnings from those contributions.

To accelerate your 401k contributions, most employers offer a matching program where they contribute money to your 401k to reflect the contributions you have made to your account. Most 401k plans have a vesting period for matching funds. In other words, you must be with the group for a certain period before you own one hundred percent of the employer's matched contributions. This vesting period can be between three to five years or more. If you leave before you are fully vested, you will forfeit the employer's matched amount, but you will retain any contributions you have made. These are the funds you can roll over as described above. Ask your employer for the vesting schedule and consult with a financial advisor to assist you with this.

Insurance

Most of the insurances, such as health, disability, dental, vision, and life insurances are self-explainable. You can choose between the cheaper HMO/MSO vs. PPO plans. Malpractice insurance is probably the most important part of this benefit package. There are two types of malpractice insurance: claims made or occurrence. Claims made are the most common type offered by employers. This insurance only covers you during the period you are employed by that employer and ends upon the termination of employment. Because of this, it is significantly cheaper than occurrence insurance. Once you leave the employment, you will need to purchase tail insurance. A tail insurance is a continuation of coverage during the same period as the claims made. An occurrence malpractice insurance includes the tail insurance and is much more expensive than the claims made. Most practices will offer an occurrence malpractice insurance. Make sure you know which is being offered.

Mentorship

Prioritize mentorship throughout your medical career. Without the guidance and support of an experienced senior physician you will get lost in the system. Mentorship is not only advantageous for clinical insight, but it is also helpful for the business of medicine. You want to work with a practice that will take you under their wings and teach you the clinical and the business side of medicine.

When I owned my practice, I had another physician who worked for me for a couple years before he decided to set up his private neonatology practice. His contract with me included a one-year noncompete clause. Despite his haste to exit my practice, he still needed to learn the business side of neonatology. A year after he left the practice, he routinely called for help setting up his practice with questions about coding and billing, employee contracts, managed care contracts, hospital contracts, and more. I gladly supported him because I wanted him to succeed. I didn't necessarily view him as a competitor, so I served as a mentor to him.

Earlier in my career, a new graduate from Texas Children's Hospital who worked for me called me for advice on a 24-week premature baby who was on a high frequency oscillatory ventilator. She mentioned that the child was dying and asked if there was anything else she could do to manage care. When I suggested systemic steroids, she quickly reminded me of the landmark study associating the use of systemic steroids with cerebral palsy in extremely low-birthweight babies. I was aware of the study and its meta-analysis study combining dozens of studies into one. I reminded her that this meta-analysis study combined small studies of severely ill babies with large studies of less severely ill babies. But there were more small studies compared to large studies in this analysis. I reiterated to her to try systemic steroids. She reluctantly got consent from the parents to do so and informed them of the risk of cerebral palsy. A few days later, she called me to say the baby responded to the steroids and had begun weaning from all support. The next month, I came on service and noticed quite a few babies on steroids. When she and I discussed the case, I reminded her that the lesson was to only use steroids when all else has failed. I reiterated that there is still a risk for cerebral palsy in this population. This was an excellent case of medical mentorship in practice to save lives.

Patient Outcomes

Prioritize working with a practice that has consistent favorable results with patients. The practice administrator or the hospital should have up-to-date outcome data that they have been tracking over time. Another source of reliable patient outcome data for physicians, hospitals, and healthcare providers is Healthgrades, a private company that conducts its own research including physician grades from patients. Also, check with state government health agencies, which are required to publish hospital outcomes and adverse effects. Ultimately, the reputation and patient outcomes for the practice you choose to work with are a reflection on you and can impact your reputation and career advancement when you move to your next job. Value-based care and quality incentives are supposed to be the future of physician compensation, but we are still far away from this.

Culture

The culture of the practice is more important than you realize. You want to feel like you are part of the family, where you can be nurtured, mentored, and valued. Consider a practice like an incubator where you can develop and grow from a young whippersnapper into an experienced physician ready to break out of your shell and fly out of the nest into new opportunities in your career.

SIGN HERE: UNDERSTANDING CONTRACTS

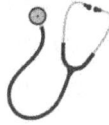

Congratulations! You've accepted your first job offer as a new physician. It's time to celebrate!

Hold on, not so fast. You're a new physician, not an attorney. You've just spent the last ten to fourteen years studying the human body and diseases, not the convoluted legal system that rules just about every aspect of life. As you take the next step to begin your career, you will wish you had some knowledge of the law, especially when you review the offer you just accepted and receive a twenty-plus-page contract to sign before starting your new job. All that legalese is intimidating. You might be tempted to view it as a bunch of gibberish and just sign the contract, but you must read it—all of it—in order to know what you're getting yourself into.

Prior to receiving your employment contract, you will receive an offer letter. The offer letter, usually a simple, one-page letter of intent (LOI), represents the employer's desire to enter into an agreement with you; that's all. It is not a commitment to join the practice. That doesn't happen until the employment contract is signed. Review the offer letter and sign it if you accept the offer as stated. Then, await the contract. This should take a few days to a few weeks.

Once you receive the employment contract, have your healthcare attorney review it thoroughly and walk you through it line by line so you understand all the terms, language, concepts, and references contained in the contract. I specify using a healthcare attorney because these professionals have an understanding of the nuances of such contracts and can help spot points in a contract that seem unusual, language that might need to be reworded, and areas that you can negotiate. Skimping on your legal support at this stage—perhaps by having an attorney friend or corporate attorney review your contract, or just deciding you can't afford legal help—will cost you in the long run . . . guaranteed. Would you go to your dermatologist for a GYN problem? Of course not. So why would you not go to a healthcare attorney for something as important as your career?

The contract is in place to protect the employer and to ensure you abide by their rules of engagement. It does not exist to satisfy your need for security. Trusting that the employer or organization you are signing on with has your best interest in mind is one of the biggest mistakes you can make at the start of your career. Remember, I made that mistake with my first job and paid a hefty price as a result. A contract is designed to protect the party that initiates it, not the person signing it. Therefore, you must be aware that your best interest might not be covered in the contract you receive. The contract is written in the best interest of the employer. And just like in a casino, the odds are with the house.

Healthcare law is unique due to the nature of the business. People's lives are at stake in the business of medicine, so contracts must be written to protect the practice, hospital, or medical group from any malfeasance that could arise. With that in mind, understand that most of the language in the healthcare contract is standard for the industry. The bigger the organization you are hired by, the less you can negotiate. However, there are some areas that you can negotiate, but typically not until later in your career when you have more to offer and leverage. Even then, do not have your attorney negotiate the contract as this can become quite expensive for you. This is when you bring in a business consultant. But not so fast. When you are just starting out in your career, you won't have the leverage for negotiations. But there are some things you can do to make sure you get what you want from your new job.

As a new physician with little room for negotiation, think of the top three priorities you want in your contract and assign a percentage weight to each one. For example, money might be number one on your list, with work/life balance and work location coming in second and third. Consider the value of the salary offered compared to the value of work hours and time off stipulated in the contract, compared to the value of your daily commute to work. If you value money 50%, work/life balance 30%, and location 20%, be certain the employment contract is in line with these priorities. Anything you want in your contract must be in writing or it doesn't exist. Verbal agreements that don't make it onto a written contract are not binding.

Once you have been in practice for a while, you can develop some leverage with your experience and business acumen: your BATNA (Best Alternative to a Negotiated Agreement). For example, if you are being hired to start a new program or take over a program, you have leverage. Obviously, they want you to run this program, so use your leverage to get more of what you want. If it's money, be prepared to have either MGMA data or tie the compensation to performance. Be reasonable and do not ask for things that could be viewed as excessive.

Practically anything can be crafted to make a deal work out for both parties, as long as it is agreed to in writing. That's where attorneys come in. Attorneys are good at writing legal documents, but they are not business people. As you progress in your career and consider owning your own practice, do not expect attorneys to develop your business plans. Hire a business consultant for that.

One of the best practices my medical consultant and I did prior to any negotiations was to role play. I would play the role of the hospital, and he would play the role of me. This exercise would help me understand their position and what they are looking for. This gave me a unique insight in how to negotiate contracts from a business perspective.

If you are at a point in your career that you have some experience to use as leverage, and you are willing to negotiate some parts of your employment contract, find out who will do the negotiations for the employer. Simply ask whoever communicates with you with the letter of intent that you want to talk about the contract. You will be put in touch with someone who will speak with you about your employment requests. This is when your attorney will step in on your behalf to clarify the language and terms of employment. I recommend that you let your attorney do this portion. Once you sign the contract, that is it. It formally ends the negotiation. Some physicians feel that by signing the contract, it is just the beginning of the continued negotiation during the first three years of employment. Not so. You are bound to this employment contract. It is a legal document, and everything you need to know about your relationship with your employer during the next three years is in your contract. Any changes made to your signed contract must be agreed on in an amendment to your contract. Any breach of the terms will result in a notice to correct the deficit, and you will have time to cure the breach as outlined in your contract.

Consider your new physician contract as a prenuptial marriage agreement. It tells you how to get in and get out of the relationship, what is required of your behavior and performance during the contract period, what compensation you can expect from your employment, and potential actions that can be taken against you should you not perform your duties as agreed. Let your attorney know about any discussions you had with the employer prior to receiving the contract. If verbal promises were made to you that do not appear in the contract, these might be points of negotiation for you. If it isn't in the contract, then you cannot count on it.

Even when you hire an attorney to review the contract, you still must review it and understand it yourself because you are the one who will be bound by the contract. Once you understand everything in the contract and you know what areas you want to negotiate, explain that to your attorney, then take yourself out of this process and let the attorney make changes to the contract as necessary. This way, your emotions and lack of legal knowledge can be kept at bay.

In the event of a question, dispute, or point of negotiation, your prospective employer will have their HR attorney communicate with you. In which case, there will be some revisions before the final version of the contract is agreed upon. Sometimes, changing a single word changes the entire meaning of a clause. For example, as a neonatologist, my employment contract should read that I am being hired as a neonatologist, not as a pediatrician. Why is this important? If the term of my employment is as a pediatrician, then my employer can utilize me as a pediatrician, which is not what I have been trained to do. Remember, you are the one who is bound by the contract once you sign it, so be certain you understand and agree to all of the terms.

A standard contract should have the following sections:

1. **Parties of the agreement:** Indicates that the agreement is entered into between you and the employer business entity with an agreement date.
2. **Witnesseth section:** Names the parties involved.
3. **Conditions precedent:** Names the following conditions that must have been satisfied before the commencement date: getting licensed in the state or privileged at the hospital; ability to obtain malpractice insurance; and ability to get a DEA, Medicare, Medicaid number. The contract will be voided if any of these conditions are not met.

4. **Purpose and employment:** Agreement between physician and employer, with the terms spelled out. The location where you are assigned to work. This should include the exact clinic or hospital, with the addresses included. Otherwise, your employer can make you work at any of their locations.

5. **Loyalty:** Commits you to work solely with the employer you are signing on with. During the term of this agreement, you are not allowed to work for other employers, including moonlighting at part-time jobs without prior authorization by your employer.

6. **Term:** Spells out the term of employment, essentially, how long the is contract for. Most contracts are for a term of one to three years. I recommend a three-year term. This gives you an opportunity to get settled into the practice, to learn the culture of the place, and to make a positive impact while there before having to reconsider your contract again.

7. **Duties:** Addresses what your schedule will be, including how many shifts, hours, or locations you will work. It also spells out responsibilities and expectations the employer has of you in addition to your work as a physician. These expectations could include being courteous and respectful to staff, completing charts and medical records within a timely manner, maintaining board eligibility or certification, attending meetings or hospital committees, notifying the employer of any potential lawsuits, and completing billing within a reasonable time.

8. **Fees:** All reimbursements or fees generated by the physician will be the property of the employer. Such fees could include reimbursement for physician services.

9. **Base compensation:** Your salary presented as a per-year sum based on the terms of the contract. An annual percentage

increase should be built in. This could range anywhere from $5,000 to $10,000 per year. You can negotiate this.

10. **Additional Shift Compensation:** If your position includes shift work, you need to have this section included in your contract. For example, if you are contracted to commit twelve 24-hour shifts, you should be paid extra for doing any additional 24-hour shifts during the year or the term of your contract. The amount per additional 24-hour shift should be stated clearly.

11. **Insurance, expenses, and fringe benefits:** This section deals with the following:

   a. Family health insurance. This is self-explanatory and non-negotiable. You will have the options of PPO, HMO, FSA.

   b. Malpractice insurance: This is a very important section. The employer will purchase malpractice insurance for you. The coverage amount should be clearly stated. It can be either an occurrence or claims made. Occurrence means that the insurance only covers you during the time you're employed by the employer. You will need a tail malpractice insurance upon your termination. Claims made means that the insurance will cover you not only during the time of employment but whenever a claim is made. Therefore, there is no need for tail malpractice insurance in this case. The contract should also spell out who is responsible for purchasing the tail malpractice insurance upon termination. This insurance can be expensive. You can negotiate inclusion of a clause stipulating that if you are terminated without cause or no fault of your own, then the employer should purchase this.

   c. Loss of professional liability insurance: This will result in immediate termination for cause. Some carriers will revoke your insurance if you have multiple malpractice cases against you.

d. Licenses, dues, and subscriptions: This should be paid for by the employer.

e. Continuing medical education: This will tell you how much the employer will pay per year for CME and what they will reimburse for. The amount can be negotiable. A new hire physician once asked me if they could use the CME money for a laptop. The employer gets to deduct the CME as an expense but cannot deduct the cost of a laptop unless it is used specifically and solely for the practice.

f. Moving expenses: The amount is agreed to in the contract and can be negotiated. What cannot be negotiated is how the amount is reimbursed. Employers usually require an invoice from a legitimate moving company, not a U-Haul shop and your family member helping you move. As stated earlier, the employer will not pay you the difference between your moving expense allotment and your actual expenses, so do not request this.

g. Retirement plan: This is standard and non-negotiable.

12. **Termination:** Pay close attention to the "for cause" and "not for cause" part of the termination clause. For cause will be defined as breach of any duties, ethics, suspension, or revocation of license or privileges, negligence, withholding professional receipts, DEA license suspension, and not completing medical records. There should be a provision about the employer providing a notice of deficiency and for you to correct the infraction defined as the cure period. You are entitled to a certain time period to cure the deficiency prior to the termination. This type of termination can be reported to the National Data Bank or to the hospital or state licensing

board. Not for cause provision is usually a notice of intent to terminate the employment. The employer will give you a period before termination, usually, one to three months. The termination clause can work in your favor as well. If you need to leave the practice, you can give your notice. Particularly, if your reason for leaving is due to some negative issues with the partners, staff, or policies, you may want to cut your losses and move on, you don't have to explain. Remember, this position will be on your resumé and future employers will ask you why you moved on. There is a good chance that they will call that practice and inquire about your employment. Don't burn bridges or trash your former employer. Be cordial and respectful on your exit.

13. **Paid vacation or sick leave:** This section should clearly outline how much time off you get between shifts, as well as for vacation, sick leave, and family leave.

14. **Non-compete covenant:** For the most part, non-compete is not enforceable, but most employers will have this provision in their contract, and they will insist that it is standard. You will have to decide to either walk away or sign the contract. If you think, since a non-compete is not enforceable then the employer can't sue you, think again. They will sue you and then you will have to hire an attorney in your defense. In most cases, you will spend a lot of time and money, and the effort won't be worth it. The time to remove any provision in the contract that is not agreeable is before you sign the contract and not after. That said, I highly recommend not challenging this provision after signing it. There are ways around this provision, such as specifying what the restrictions are with locations. For example, as a neonatologist, I shouldn't be restricted to practicing pediatrics in an outpatient setting. The restriction should extend to five miles from my primary

hospital, not the entire city or state. There is also a provision that allows you to buy out your noncompete. There is a calculation that is agreed upon in the contract as to what this amount of the buy-out will be. Usually, it is a percentage of your salary. It shouldn't be so huge that it's impossible to achieve. This is a lot cheaper than paying an attorney $500 an hour to defend you.

15. **Non-solicitation:** If you leave the practice, you may not entice or take away the employer's current staff or physicians to form another competing practice. There is usually a time limit to this. So, after a year or two, you should be free to solicit employees to work for you.

16. **Arbitration:** There are several arbitration associations. Once activated, the employer is the entity that will assign the arbitrator. The arbitrator will serve as a mediator between you and your employer. Consult your healthcare attorney about the pros and cons of each type of arbitrator.

17. **Confidentiality:** Stipulates that you will keep confidential every part of the business from billing to medical records, malpractice suits, hiring practices, communications, and anything else related to how the practice operates. This clause typically has an expiration, often two to three years following an employee's departure. Earlier in the book I mentioned a physician who had a gag clause in his contract that prevented him from telling me all the negatives about the practice I joined. This provision covers that.

18. **Partnership:** Some practices offer partnership as part of the agreement. If this is the case, seek the advise of a healthcare business consultant in addition to your healthcare attorney. There are many types of partnership; most will have a buy-in phrase which allows you to buy into a practice or business. Some will allow sweat equity after serving a predetermined

amount of time with the practice. The advantage for the employer to allow you to become a partner is so you can share expenses and overhead. If you are willing to take some of the risks, the incentive for you is to keep overhead to a minimum. Sometimes, remaining an employee with a guaranteed income and no risk is best. The last thing you want to be is a partner with an employee attitude.

Different employers will have different templates for employment contracts. They will always tell you that theirs is a standard contract. However, there are usually areas you can request to be revised. Communicate with your attorney and get them to change the wording to accomplish what you want. Remember the three things that are important to you with the weighted percentage mentioned earlier. Be willing to walk away if you don't get what was promised. It is much better to do this at the beginning of the relationship than to end up with litigation and bad blood later.

The Carrots

Some employers will dangle carrots in front of you to get you to sign on. Don't be too hasty to fall for the dangling carrots, though. Step back and ask yourself why they are offering certain benefits.

Offering a bonus for passing your boards to become certified is not unheard of. Request this upfront in your employment contract. When in private practice, I always included this in contracts with my new graduates. However, I never offered these bonuses for recertification. Don't get greedy.

An employer might offer to pay off your student loans. This is common in military or rural contracts and can be an attractive offer to explore. As exciting as this might sound though, tread with caution. Examine this kind of offer to determine what you will have to give up to obtain this benefit. Will you have to commit to a specified number of years with this employer? The most common requirement for such a benefit usually involves at least three to five years commitment to the job. Military contracts will be longer.

The bottom line is, be cautious of special offers. There is always a reason employers dangle these carrots in front of you. Be smart and find out why, then make the decision that works best for you and your career goals.

Orientation: Your First Day On the Job

Now that you have signed your employment contract and you're hired, what's next? You will now be inundated with a lot of paperwork. Most of which will be your responsibility to complete in a timely manner. Your employment start date depends on how quickly you can complete all the necessary credentialing, which means you will not get paid until you start working. Additionally, you must get the following prior to starting work: your state licensing, federal DEA number, federal Medicaid/Medicare number, hospital privileges, malpractice insurance, benefit enrollment, EMR enrollment/orientation, billing and coding orientation, insurance plans enrollment, compliance training, hospital orientation, and procedure competency.

I have seen several new hires having to walk their application for state licensing to the different offices at the state capitol to expedite the approval process. You're out of luck with the federal part. July is when new residents start; therefore, all these state and federal agencies are extremely busy. Download a good photo app on your phone that allows you to take pictures of required documents. Scan and convert them to a PDF file to send by email. Get your passport photo early and have enough copies for your application. Some agencies require a black and white photo; some require a color photo. Read the instructions carefully before submitting your application.

Now that you have completed all the requirements for employment, you are ready for your first day on the job. Here are a few things to keep in mind during orientation:

- **Do the right thing.** This applies to patient care and business life. Don't let money drive patient care. Don't let other people or staff tell you how to care for your patient. You and your patient should be involved in the management and care of the patient. Lots of offices have a list of procedures or labs for you to order during an office visit, especially offices that have in-house laboratories. This is for revenue-generating purposes. Don't overdo it. Focus only on tests and procedures that are necessary. Overcharging is committing fraud.

- **Be a good communicator.** Not only to your patient but also to the staff and your colleagues. Explain things plainly and simply. Speak slowly and avoid using medical jargon or abbreviations with your patient. Make sure the patient understands what you are saying. I find that good communication avoids lawsuits. Don't hide anything. Be as transparent as possible. Above all, keep your word. Trust must be earned, but it is easily destroyed once it is lost.

- **Be genuine and respectful to everyone.** You don't know what someone is going through, so practice kindness and patience. But also, be stern. You are the one directing the care of your patient. Let the family be part of the management, but do not allow them to direct the patient's care. Empathy will go a long way when dealing with families. The same goes for the staff. If they don't like you, they will make life difficult for you.

- **Learn the business.** Get to know how the practice functions. From the front office to the back office. How does billing work? What happens to a claim once you submit the charges? How do you get paid by insurance? What is the self-pay policy? What are managed care contracts? What are the over-head expenses of the practice?

- **Be honest.** Lying is a breach of trust that I don't tolerate. Doctors are not immune to lying. I have witnessed it many times. If you lie to the hospital or staff, they will catch you and you will be disciplined by the hospital or medical staff. Never falsify records because this is grounds for termination.

- **Ask questions.** No one in charge expects you to know every-thing. They do, however, expect you to ask questions; anything from clinical to business. As mentioned, enlist a mentor that you can ask questions of.

- **Set expectations on day one.** If the employer doesn't set expectations, then you need to ask. What are your boundaries? Can you leave early if there are no patients to be seen? How is time off and vacation time granted? Who does the approval? How far in advance do these requests need to be submitted?

- **Avoid compromising situations.** As a male doctor, do not walk into a patient's room without a chaperone, especially if the patient identifies as female. When it comes down to your word against someone else's, you will lose. Do not make personal advancements toward other staff, regardless of their position. Office romances can be distracting at best if they work out, and disastrous at worst if they don't. Keep your per-sonal information—phone number, address, financial, etc.—private from coworkers. Refrain from gossip. Never use the hospital equipment or supplies for personal purposes.

Despite all the warnings above, starting this new phase of your career and life should be exciting. Just by reading this book you will show up on day one of your new job smarter than most physicians. Do your part to remain diligent and observant. And always remember why you entered the field of medicine to begin with.

LIVING LARGE? AVOID THE TRAP— LIFE OF A DOCTOR

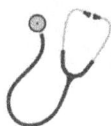

You're in. Yes, you've survived the interview and the onboarding for your new job. You are seeing patients regularly, completing paperwork, engaging with the staff, even getting high-fives from management. You are officially a doctor. You are now a pillar of the community. And here is where many new physicians blow it.

If you are like most professionals new to the medical industry, you are likely earning the largest salary you've ever earned. You can now afford to buy all sorts of items you've dreamed of—from a luxury car and designer clothes to expensive jewelry and a mansion—but don't get ahead of yourself. Don't let your new job, title, and lifestyle fully encompass you. On the flip side, you might be still holding onto the mindset of a student: the free-flowing life of the party who has few responsibilities and says and does whatever you like, whenever you like. The reality check is that some of the things you did as a student, you cannot do as an employed physician. You have responsibilities now. You have a reputation to uphold. You must have some balance. And that balance is essentially between your professional life and your personal life. Both are equally important.

You have spent the last ten to fourteen years learning your craft. Now you should learn how the business and the politics of medicine work together. Believe me, there are plenty of politics in medicine, whether you realize it or like it or not. Start now to understand the intricacies of the practice, hospital, or organization you work for. Yes, even as you tend to patients and manage reports and other administrative duties, you still have to be involved in the operations as required by your employer. Attend hospital committee, department, and medical staff meetings. Listen to what is discussed. This will give you a fair idea of what the dynamics are and who the players are. Believe me, your employer will be paying attention to which physicians are participating in these meetings. Your attendance and active involvement are crucial to your personal brand and career advancement.

On the personal side, remember that your career shouldn't be the only important thing in your life. Go back and review the chapter titled "New Physician, Know Thyself" and review these areas: Define Your Career Goals, Explore Your Priorities, Establish Your Personal Brand and Ethics, and Know Your Self-Worth. Now is the time to get to know who you are. Take the next three years to do this. As you navigate the landscape of your career, you must also find personal life balance: relationships, time management, family, stress relief, hobbies, fitness, mindless activities, entertainment, friendships, charity, faith.

At the end of the day, family and your mental health should matter most. Whether you are single, divorced, dating, engaged, or married, be sure to surround yourself with people you love and trust. I cannot emphasize this enough. There will be days when your job will beat you down emotionally. Having a loving support system to lean on and a stable mental disposition will get you through the most difficult days. Sometimes, family and spouses aren't enough. Do not hesitate to seek help. During my divorce, I visited a psychologist weekly, and it was a lifesaver. I discovered a lot about myself during those sessions. Sometimes people on the outside can see things more clearly than you can see for yourself. If you seek help, remember that everything you say during these sessions is protected under privacy laws and client privileges.

Find a hobby to take your mind off of your job. Don't let your entire day be consumed by your clinical duties. If you do, you will get burned out in no time. Workout in the gym, hire a personal trainer, join a social club, learn to cook, go fishing or hunting. Anything physically or mentally active that will get you out of the clinic or hospital and clear your mind will benefit you. About fifteen years into owning my private practice, I began to use cooking as a hobby and a form of stress relief, and I still do. It offered a mental release and a way to turn off the critical thinking part of my brain and develop the creative side.

Avoid turning to frequent late-night partying and drinking as your release activity. It's okay to blow off some steam every now and then in moderation, but doing this too often could eventually affect your job and your reputation. As a physician, you will get invited to many events. Some are just to mix and mingle. Some will be for charity, other might be formal events. Diversify your surroundings to stay well grounded.

One of the biggest blind spots new physicians have is a lack of financial education. This is true in many other fields as well, as the American education system does a poor job of providing instruction on personal finance. If you do not already have a trusted financial institution prior to starting your new job, get set up with one. At the very least, establish a personal checking account and a self-directed brokerage account for investments. Once a bank knows you're a physician they will bend over backward to introduce you to their line of products, from credit cards, a line of credit, or a loan, to a certified financial advisor to assist with investments.

Whether through your bank or through references from trusted friends or family, find a good financial advisor to help manage your money. But do not let this financial advisor completely handle your finances. They work for a financial institution and often earn a commission on products they recommend. What you need is trusted advice and guidance, not someone who sees you as a walking dollar sign. Even when you hire a financial advisor, you should continuously learn about finances, such as various types of accounts, investment vehicles, and terminology. Go online and visit YouTube or Reddit or join an investment club. Learn to manage your own money. Don't depend solely on your financial advisor. Educate yourself financially. Don't get into debt unless it's good debt, like buying a house with a mortgage. Start investing for the future.

Learn about tax deductions. As a W-2 employee, you won't be able to deduct any tax liabilities. So, what do you do? Max out your 401k. Get a 529 plan for your kid's future education. Buy real estate and depreciate it. Deduct the property tax, mortgage, and any improvements on your residence or rental property. Take advantage of the lower interest rates for doctors from the bank. Form a living revocable trust for your family. Learn to create generational wealth like the Vanderbilts have done through life insurance paid to the trust. Establish a will to avoid probate court in the future. These are but a few strategies for success. Hire a good CPA and estate attorney to help you.

Your salary as a physician is among the highest of most professional careers. That salary might seem like a lot of money now, but here's the thing: You won't be practicing medicine forever, so do what you can to make your money last a lifetime and support a comfortable lifestyle for you and your family for years to come. In addition to learning about investing your money for the long term, learn to budget and live within your means now. This means managing your lifestyle so that your monthly expenses are reasonable and affordable and leave a sizable amount left over for saving and investing. Don't go out and buy the most expensive car or house. Don't go crazy spending on lavish gifts for friends and family or extravagant luxury travel, at least not right away. Play your cards right and there will be plenty of time for the luxury experience. For now, avoid an excessive lifestyle, and scrutinize expenses deliberately. There are plenty of physicians living from paycheck to paycheck. I know quite a few who have had to delay retirement as a result of poor financial choices early in their career. In fact, there were quite a few physicians on my payroll who would ask for an advance on their pay to help make ends meet. Bad habits are hard to change. So, apply good financial finance practices early in your career and keep at it.

The same goes for buying different insurances. There will be opportunities to buy life insurance, disability insurance, health insurance, homeowner's insurance, umbrella insurance, and more. Your employer will most likely provide term life insurance, short-term disability insurance, and malpractice insurance. Life insurance is your responsibility. A complicated subset of insurance unto itself, life insurance includes term, whole, universal, or variable life insurance. They each serve a different purpose. Disability insurances are either short-term or long-term disability. Health insurance will offer you PPO, HMO, or HSA. With homeowner's insurance, you can adjust your payout by changing the deductible and/or the premium you pay.

Umbrella insurance is something you should get if you have significant assets like a big house. This is to protect you from frivolous lawsuits that are unrelated to malpractice. For example, if someone has an accident in your front yard and decides to sue you (and they likely will when they find out you are a physician), you don't want to lose everything you've worked so hard for. You should also consider supplemental insurances, which offer additional coverage to your standard health insurance. Which type of supplemental insurance you choose depends on your current life circumstances. If you are single with no children and have few assets, supplemental insurance may be all you need. If you are married, you need to consider your spouse. What happens if you die or become disabled? If you also have children, supplemental insurance is essential. AFLAC offers an excellent product and is portable, which means you can take it with you when you change jobs.

Protecting your assets while you are alive and after you are gone is essential for any professional. Unfortunately, far too many physicians neglect to properly do so. Consult with a wealth management group or an estate attorney for details on wills, trusts, and other options to protect your assets. Unfortunately, as a physician, you will become a target for frivolous lawsuits, so learn what you can now about asset protection and take action as you build your wealth.

Don't get drawn into tax schemes to reduce taxes. In the beginning of your career is not the time to be thinking about this. Maybe when you have gained enough assets then you can consult with CPA that deal with high net-worth individuals. Then you can entertain things like 1031 exchanges, purchasing tax credits, 529 college savings plans, agricultural tax exemptions, and other more complex tax sheltering opportunities.

Surround yourself with people you can trust and depend on. If you are married, your spouse should be your primary emotional support mechanism. Be grateful for that support because you will need it when work becomes hectic and stressful. Some days you will come home and have lots to complain about. Be sure your spouse understands that and you work together to come up with ways to deal with it. Simply dumping all your frustrations on your spouse is fruitless and a recipe for disaster. Instead, use those conversations as a form of release. Share your frustrations and then let it go. If you are single, be careful of fake people on social media. They will direct message you and request to be your friend, then tempt you into sending money or developing a relationship. Trust, but verify. It's hard to meet people outside of the hospital setting, but pay attention before getting serious with anyone. If there are red flags about a person you are dating, do not ignore them. Hire a private detective to verify what the information they tell you before proceeding any further. You may be surprised with what you find out. There are lots of people looking for a status upgrade. So look before crossing that street. And if you find that you can't live without this person, get a prenuptial agreement.

Friendships are also critical as you progress through your career. It's important to have friends in the medical field, but also equally important to have friends outside of the field. Keep your circle small and be sure it includes people you can trust and confide in. You are human with emotions and feelings, so curate a small circle of trusted friends you can rely on for emotional support.

Being a physician carries with it a certain degree of privilege and respect. That is the upside. But you are human as well. Mental health is important. Most employers offer mental health support through their insurance. Access this support as often as needed and do not let stressful situations or emotional concerns pile up unaddressed, whether personal or professional. When I was a pediatric resident, I learned that a well-respected OB resident didn't report to duty. He was jovial and fun to work with, and I had worked with him just a few nights before on call at the hospital. I went to his apartment with several colleagues. What we found was shocking. He was in the bathtub full of water and had cut both radial arteries. He had also injected himself with heparin to prevent his blood from clotting. From the looks of things, it was clear that he had thought of the suicide well in advance. We later learned that his wife had left him. We had no idea of his dire emotional state. To this day, the thought of this tragedy, and how detailed his plan was, still sends chills down my spine.

Serving patients and your community as a physician is both an honor and a huge responsibility. Do not take it lightly. Society places a lot of trust and value on doctors, and rightly so; we hold people's lives in our hands. Do your best to maintain a balanced mindset and remain grateful for all that you know, do, and have.

SAGE WISDOM

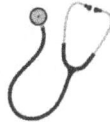

Chances are, I have been in the medical field longer than you have been alive. Over more than three decades, my medical career has allowed many opportunities. I have mastered my craft and have a keen understanding of the business of medicine. It doesn't matter if it's neonatology or any other specialty; the business of medicine is the same. It's all about the profits and losses, relationships and politics.

At each level of my career, I have learned valuable lessons. From the beginning of my career, I learned about tail malpractice insurance. Although I believed my employer should have told me about this, I learned the hard way of the importance of this crucial coverage. It was a hard and expensive lesson, and I have never forgotten it. The lesson here is to cover yourself with the proper insurance at the start of your career. Later in my career, I had to add umbrella insurance, insurance for Director and Officer (D+O), workers compensation insurance, errors and omission insurance, and more. All of this came about because I took the risk to start my own private practice. Is this something you should do?

Going Solo

You may decide to be a solo practitioner and open your own private practice. As someone who has been down that road, I would advise against it. In my former practice, I served as the CEO and the COO of my practice from 2000 to 2017. Things were different back then. For example, there were no electronic medical record (EMR) requirements, no pharmaco rules, no compliance, and no Health Insurance Portability and Accountability Act of 1996 (HIPAA). Now, the overhead and the regulatory requirements are overwhelming: EMR to HR and compliance officer, new software and hardware to satisfy all these requirements, 24/7 technical support needed for the software, T1 internet line to prevent hackers from breaking into your server, and the cybersecurity software. All of this costs money.

There are a lot of details that come with owning your own practice, like knowing that parents have up to thirty days to put their newborn baby onto their insurance plan or on Medicaid; that hospitals usually put the mother's insurance information on the baby's fact sheet and will correct it within three weeks, once they know the correct insurance information. So, if the billing company submits the claim too early, it will be denied by the insurance company. Doing eighty percent of the work upfront leaves only twenty percent for you to follow up with on the back end. Asking for the aging AR (accounts receivables) by 30 days, 60 days, 90 days and greater than 120 days buckets will help you understand how well your billing company is doing. Your collections rate doesn't give you enough data to determine whether or not your hard work is yielding any results. That's the way things should work.

Another tip is avoid submitting claims too quickly during the first half of the year when everything goes to deductibles. Wait till everyone else's claims go to deductible. It's much tougher to collect from a patient who doesn't understand that the deductibles are the patient's responsibility. Instead, submit your claims faster during the latter half of the year after deductibles have been met. This significantly increases your chances of being paid by the insurance carrier.

Starting my own practice was one of the most exhilarating and challenging parts of my medical career. By the time I got to this point in my career I had learned a lot about the business of medicine. Now, I was ready to put it to the test. That's when I realized how little I knew and how much I still needed to learn. If you decide that owning a practice is for you, hire a medical consultant to set up the practice. They will help with setting up the software and hardware, as well as hiring the front and back office staff. Additionally, they will set up the billing and collection with either an in-house or an outside billing company, connect you with an answering service, and help with managed care contracts. When you establish your own private practice, you are officially an entrepreneur, and your responsibilities and stress level will multiply faster than you could ever imagine. No matter what happens in your practice, as the owner you are ultimately responsible for everything in the office. You should know and be in control of every aspect of how the office works and the workflow within your business.

One of the most difficult challenges of owning a medical practice is finding good employees to staff your practice. I went through a lot of different office managers and was never able to find the perfect one. It turns out that I know more about the business than anyone I hired. The reality is that you will never find someone for any position who understands and cares about your business as much as you do. For them it's just a job, a means to earn an income so they can feed their family. Don't ever lose sight of that. Vet each new hire properly and respect the experience and skills they bring to the practice. When you do find good people, pay them well. Avoid hiring family members who don't know anything about medical practice. You can't fire them if they are your spouse, sibling, cousin, or parent.

Learning about billing and collections was extremely difficult for me. There are plenty of mom-and-pop revenue cycle companies that will happily offer their services to you. I highly recommend you visit their place of business. I interviewed one company that charged a small fee for processing claims. It turns out it was operating out of a garage. Bigger companies can be better, but they tend to have a lot of clients. If you are a small client, you might get lost in the weeds. It is your responsibility to learn about billing and collections.

During the peak of my private practice, I employed two in-house legal counsels. It was the best decision for the practice. They protected the practice from frivolous lawsuits on many occasions. They also protected the practice with all the necessary insurances. At first, I thought those insurances were a waste of money, but they did come in handy. Those lawsuits taught me to never talk to anyone about business without one of my attorneys present to take notes. One day, my head of HR called me before payroll and asked if I had authorized a $5,000 one-time bonus to a physician. He had said I told him this in passing. Of course, that conversation never occurred. That experience taught me to record all board meetings with partners and associates.

For entrepreneurs, it's not about the money, but more about the idea of being your own boss, calling your own shots, building something from nothing, innovating, and recognizing and capitalizing on opportunities. Some of the more notable contemporary entrepreneurs include Elon Musk and Steve Jobs. Money wasn't the motivator for either of them. Instead, their incentive was to see their ideas come to life. Because they never gave up on any of those concepts much of our society has benefitted from their vision. Look at how much Elon Musk spent to purchase Twitter. He spent $43 billion, fired three-quarters of the employees, then operated the company better and more efficiently than it had ever been run before.

> *If you are fortunate to find a good attorney,*
> *keep them near.*

After the sale of my business, I was inundated with lawsuits. I had seven lawsuits from former business associates and doctors wanting a piece of the pie. I was shocked and disgusted with this. Some wanted just a few thousand dollars to go away. Some wanted a percentage of the sale. Thankfully, I had a great attorney. One by one, he either got the lawsuits thrown out or countered sue them and went to deposition. A good attorney is worth their weight in gold. But beware of the games some attorneys will play. You will be shocked by their fees and fee structure. You might pay a high hourly fee for using a partner in a law firm, then pay a separate hourly fee for work done for you by a junior associate at the firm. What they don't tell you is that the partner and junior associate will meet weekly and both will bill you at the same time. So, you end up paying for both attorneys to review your single case at the same time. This happened to me on more than one occasion. An attorney told me once that it's not about the law or justice. It's about winning the game. To many, the means justify the ends. Attorneys think in a "yes or no" linear way, black or white. This is a different mindset than physicians. We think in pathways. Most cases will get settled out of court, but your attorney will most likely make you go through discovery and then maybe arbitration before talking about settling. Remember that it's a business for them too. If you are fortunate to find a good attorney, keep them near.

Marriages are difficult and even more so when you run a busy medical practice. Any marriage therapist or couple who has been married for decades will tell you that both partners must spend time working on the marriage. That means prioritizing your relationship even as you build your career. When you have children, they also require your love and attention. Spend time with your family because they need you as much as your patients and employer do. The bonus is that they also love you and want the best for you. Therefore, always place your family first because the alternative can be devastating and have long-lasting negative effects.

Going through a divorce was probably the toughest time of my life. I was depressed and mentally exhausted. Divorce attorneys can be vicious and inhuman in their efforts to do their job and extract as much as they can for their client. The bottom line in divorce proceedings is that it's business and not personal. If you are facing divorce, take care of yourself first. This too shall pass. My divorce was one of the primary reasons I sold my practice. Consider a prenuptial agreement before the wedding, especially if you are already established and have assets to protect. If you have significant assets, think about estate planning with trust funds for the kids and advance tax planning.

My decision to sell the practice was probably one of the hardest things I had to do besides writing this book. After all, the practice was my baby for seventeen years—the good, the bad and the ugly of it—but I was exhausted, both mentally and physically. It wasn't fun going to work and facing the relentless stress of HR and payroll, then going home to a mess. Only a few individuals within the practice knew any of this because I kept it to myself. My colleagues in the practice probably thought I was greedy and a sellout, but I had had enough. I was ready to get out even though I didn't know what was in store for me in the future. I was relieved after the sale was announced, but then I thought, *What have I done?* One year later, my main hospital in Houston was purchased by HCA Healthcare. The medical staff there all thought I had inside information of the pending sale to HCA. I didn't. Another year later, HCA announced the closure of this same hospital. Once again, I had phone calls from the medical staff. Did I know this in advance? How can I be that lucky twice? I truly believe that everything works out in the end. When one door closes, another opens.

Thanks to all I have learned over my thirty years in the medical profession—and perhaps despite all my mistakes—I succeeded. I sold my practice to a national company. I got remarried and joined a renown Children's Hospital in South Carolina, serving as medical director for all their community hospitals. I developed an innovative neonatal telemedicine program for the Children's Hospital and am developing a neonatal hospitalist program. And now, I am sharing my experience with you in this book to provide helpful insights for your career.

Secrets to My Success: It ain't easy being me

By now, you might think it sounds pretty great to be Dr. Giep. But wait! There's more to the story than you realize. It isn't easy being me. However, I have had great successes.

Want to know how to be a Dr. Giep? Here are a few secrets to my success:

1. **Luck.** You will need a lot of luck to be successful. You may start off with the ideal job thanks to the recommendation of a mentor or colleague. I call that good luck. Sometimes it's smarter to be lucky than it is lucky to be smart. But the ideal job may still fail. Or you might join a practice or a hospital and within a short period of time, it is bought out by a larger entity. Soon after, they close or consolidate. That could leave you searching for a new job. That's bad luck. Or, on the personal side, you go through a nasty divorce and lose half of the wealth you worked so hard to build. That's bad luck. You will find luck around every corner. Beware of the bad and celebrate the good. My wife tells me that in order to bring luck and good fortune to yourself, you have to do charity and do good to others. This is an Asian belief. I believe that there is something to it. Don't expect good things to happen right away. People ask me all the time. Why am I still working

after selling my practice? I tell them I work now because I enjoy it and because it's going to bring good karma not for me but for my family and their future.

2. **Prioritize work/life balance.** Being a physician can be a tough job with long hours and lots of stress. Staying sharp and attentive all the time while lacking sleep and rest can be daunting and wear anyone down. That ongoing fatigue can affect your quality of life, which diminishes your work/life balance. Find activities to help manage stress. Prioritize your relationships, your health (physical, mental, and emotional), and your environment. My health and fitness routine includes a daily supplement of Vitamin D and magnesium, as well as drinking hot green tea and some freshly squeezed lemon slices every morning to detox. Also, I go to a gym with a personal trainer every day for an hour. Above all, take care of yourself first.

3. **Serve your customers.** Business is all about relationships and knowing what the customers want. The customers in this case are your patients, their families, your staff, and hospital administrators. Learn what the customers want and do your best to provide the service and information needed to satisfy their needs without compromising your ethics or well-being. It doesn't matter what business you're in; it's all about relationships. Above all don't make promises you can't keep. Your word is your bond. Early in my career, I was approached by the CEO of a Houston hospital and we negotiated a deal for my group to take over the neonatal ICU in just four months. I asked to see the service contract before I began recruiting. He stood there in front of half of dozen people and said "My word is my bond. Plus, all these people will serve as my witnesses." With that, I started the recruitment process and hired two new physicians for the hospital.

Six weeks before the start of the contract, the CEO stopped returning my phone calls. I knew then the jig was up. Turns out the CEO had used me as leverage to get a better deal with the existing physician group. He never apologized or returned any of my calls. This was poor integrity on his part and a terrible way to serve his customers. This is not how you conduct business.

4. **Be willing to take risks.** People who are not willing to take risks become stuck in their own nightmare of a career and are unable to break free from their situation. They complain to their colleagues, but never realize that the solution lies in taking thoughtful risks—even small ones—to improve their lives. Taking risks can be scary, but not taking chances will keep you stuck where you are. I have known plenty of physicians who were unable or unwilling to take that first step toward something new or better either because of fear of failure or because of lack of self-confidence.

5. **Maintain a strong marriage and home life.** Having a strong marriage makes a big difference. It's the foundation from which you can build a career. Keep your house in order. If it's in disarray, you won't be able to focus on building a career. It will drag you down. If you are not married before adding M.D. to your name, consider getting a prenup before saying "I do." Once you are married, continue to work on the marriage and keep it fresh. If or when you have children, prioritize spending time with them. I know plenty of physicians going through divorce who contemplated suicide as a way out. Martial arts legend Bruce Lee is known for his advice when facing life's difficulties: "Do not pray for an easy life. Pray for the strength to endure a difficult one."

6. **Manage your money.** Get a good financial advisor and banker. Without one, you won't be able to get the credit you

need to fund any venture. Without funding you won't go far. A bank will jump at the opportunity to work with a physician because they are aware of your income potential. Learn about finances and investments so you don't end up being among the many physicians living paycheck to paycheck. Don't depend solely on your financial advisor and banker. They work for someone and will steer you toward their institution's recommended products.

7. **Become aware of your own self-worth.** You will learn this over time. As you grow your experience, your worth and value also grow. This can happen through knowledge, specialization, personality, insight, or integrity. Get a mentor and learn from them.

WHAT'S NEXT?

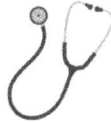

Rather than begin your career in medicine clueless, like I did, let this book be a beginning guide as you navigate your job search and learn the business of medicine. You have learned your clinical skills through your training. Hopefully, this book will give you more insight into what lies ahead. Here are my thoughts about some promising opportunities in the medical field.

The Future of Medicine

With all the doom and gloom, there is a ray of sunshine on the horizon. The COVID-19 pandemic ushered in the era of telemedicine, an innovation that gave providers and insurers an alternative to traditional medical care. Over the next few decades, the practice of medicine will become increasingly virtual, aided by digital technologies like artificial intelligence, telehealth, and wearable devices. Harvard Medical School professor Jagmeet Singh is witnessing many of these changes firsthand. His new book, *Future Care: Sensors, Artificial Intelligence, and the Reinvention of Medicine,* draws from his work as a cardiologist, his research into device technologies, and his own experience being hospitalized with COVID-19 to explore the rapidly changing healthcare landscape.

Telemedicine could revolutionize the healthcare industry and become the answer for more work/life balance for many physicians. Insurance companies are now reimbursing physician fees for telehealth, which supports the push to make this innovation an essential component of the AMA Recovery Plan for America's Physicians. Telemedicine is critical to the future of healthcare, which is why the AMA continues to lead the charge to aggressively expand telehealth policy, research, and resources to ensure physician practice sustainability and fair payment. Coverage parity requires payers to cover the cost of a service via telehealth if it is also covered in-person and can be delivered remotely while meeting the standard of care. As of January 2024, more than forty states had a telehealth coverage parity law on the books and twenty-one had implemented payment parity. In addition, various types of payment parity bills were introduced in fifteen states in 2024.

Artificial intelligence (AI) is another exciting change coming to healthcare. AI already allows large hospital systems to link their large electronic health records via EMS like EPIC, Meditech, or Cerner. We are still very early in the AI revolution; therefore, there are many challenges ahead that will likely come with increased regulation. The difficulties that AI presents currently are ethical and data privacy issues. There are also concerns about biases with AI. If the data set to train AI is flawed or impartial then biases will occur. Despite this, I believe AI will ultimately revolutionize the healthcare industry. AI can fill many gaps and play many roles. Algorithms already work well for several areas of medicine, such as the diagnosis of diabetic retinopathy via evaluation of images of the retina.

These two new frontiers—telemedicine and artificial intelligence—will improve workflow and relieve work-related stress and staffing shortages.

As for Me . . .

After selling my practice, I retired for five months and came out of retirement due to boredom and not having a well-planned exit strategy. After all, medicine is all I know. So, I accepted a new position with a children's hospital as the medical director running all their community-based nurseries outside of the children's hospital. I developed a unique telehealth model using telemedicine to co-manage Level-2 and Level-1 nurseries in rural communities with neonatal nurse practitioners and pediatricians. I am blessed to be working with a good group of physicians and an institution that believes in my vision for the community.

Now, I am working on more hobbies outside of medicine, including doing more charity work. Writing this book has truly been the toughest thing I have done outside of medicine. I also truly believe in karma. Things happen for a reason. When one door closes, another one opens. Just make sure when the door closes, nail it shut. Don't look back. I would never have imagined after my divorce and selling my business that I would be where I am at today. Thank you for reading this life journey of mine. I hope you have found it helpful and that it assists you in creating a career in the business of medicine that sustains you and your family, that serves patients with integrity, and that offers you a sense of pride and satisfaction for years to come.

I want to leave you with a few books I recommend if you want to succeed in business.

1. *The Art of War* by Sun Tsu
2. *The Prince* by Niccolo Machiavelli
3. *Winning* by Jack Welch
4. *How to Read People Like a Book* by James W. Williams
5. *Be Water, My Friend: The Teachings of Bruce Lee* by Shannon Lee

Lastly, I want to leave you with this quote from Bruce Lee.

"If you always put limits on what you can do, physical or anything else, it'll spread over into the rest of your life. There are no limits, there are only plateaus. A man must constantly exceed his level. You reach your full potential once you don't believe your limiting beliefs."

ABOUT THE AUTHOR

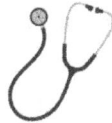

The son of a physician and the eldest of four boys who all grew up to become doctors, Dr. Tung Giep knew early on what his career path would look like. He always wanted to make a difference in the lives of patients and to help shape the future of the healthcare system. The experience of emigrating from Vietnam to the US after the Vietnam War strengthened his resolve and built a resilience that he has carried throughout his life and career.

Dr. Giep is a graduate of Wofford College in Spartanburg, SC. He received his medical degree and completed residency at The Medical University of South Carolina (MUSC), then went on to complete his fellowship at Children's Mercy Hospital in Kansas City, MO. His background includes board certification in pediatrics and neonatal-perinatal medicine, a fellow with the American Academy of Pediatrics, and over twenty-five years serving as a medical director within community hospitals. He founded and served as the president of NICS, providing hospitals with 24/7 Level-2 and Level-3 NICU and pediatric hospitalist programs for seventeen years before the company was sold to a national company in 2017.

Throughout his career, he successfully developed and scaled neonatal programs from the ground up, providing innovative and quality-focused patient care and resulting in profitability and streamlined processes. Under his leadership, several underperforming nurseries have been transformed into high-performing and top-producing units within a short turnaround time. Additionally, he has led the initiative to implement an innovative telemedicine program via Teledoc that provides clinicians 24/7 access to neonatologists, helping to avoid unnecessary transfers and provide more comprehensive care.

He is the Medical Director of Community Hospital Level-2 Nurseries for a Children's Hospital-affiliated hospital, where he manages the development of the Neonatal Telemedicine Program.

He credits much of his success to a diverse background that includes clinical, business, and financial expertise, along with his innate ability to cultivate meaningful relationships with both internal and external stakeholders. His focus on a collaborative and integrated approach to creating a seamless and best-in-class healthcare experience for all—with the patient and the families at the forefront—has been at the core of his entire career as a healthcare provider.

Dr. Giep lives in Houston, TX with his wife, Michelle and sons Sebastian and Benjamin, and enjoys travel, cooking, and keeping up with the latest technology developments in the medical field. He insists that writing this book has been one of the hardest things he has ever done in life.

ACKNOWLEDGMENTS

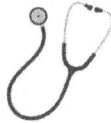

I want to thank Dr. R. T. Hall, the "father of neonatology" in the midwest, for giving me the opportunity in neonatology to train with him and learn the skills that I have today. Without him, I would not have become the clinician that I am today.

Sincere gratitude goes to my mom who raised four boys to become physicians. Without the constant tiger Asian mom, I would not be the individual I am today. Mom, you were the disciplinarian we needed and you kept us on a straight path without straying.

To my dad, who provided the inspiration I needed to keep going in my career when I wanted to quit. By telling me to look in the mirror to see that maybe the problem was me and not everyone else, he inspired me to not fail and to be a unique game changer in all areas of my life.

Thanks goes to Dr. H. Donald Dobbs, former professor of biology at Wofford College in Spartanburg, South Carolina, for molding minds and shaping brains.

Also, I want to acknowledge Jim Ramsey, my family business consultant. Over the years, I have enjoyed our discussions about what went wrong and right with the practice, the many people you had to let go, your obsession with *The Godfather* movie, and your comparison of me to Michael Corleone. Thank you for the challenges and the rewards.

Much appreciation goes to thank Joe Taylor and associates for helping me through the toughest part of the history of my business. Without the corporate retreats and corporate rules and regulations, I would be ruined. Thank you for helping me throughout the tough times and the good times.

Thanks also to those who agreed to read an early version of the manuscript for this book: Kristina Manning, Austin Rutledge, and Peter Maurides Your feedback and insights are greatly appreciated and helped improve the final content to make it more digestible and beneficial for the intended reader.

Tung with wife, Michelle and sons Sebastian and Benjamin

To my wife Michelle, thank you for believing in me and taking in a downtrodden soul at my lowest point. You made me believe in karma and myself again. For that, I am eternally grateful.

To my son Sebastian, may light shine on your path and lead you to be wise and successful in whatever path you take. I am always proud of you.

To my son Benjamin, follow your own path, wherever it leads you.

Lastly, I want to thank God for granting me the wisdom, the good fortune/luck, the health, and the knowledge for me to do what I do day in and day out in taking care of sick newborns and in business.

Dr. Giep speaks widely about the business of medicine.
He is available for lectures and educational
instruction for new graduates.
He consults with hospitals on their existing or
future nursery business.

To hire him to speak, or to schedule him for interviews
on podcasts, TV, or radio shows,
contact info@thebusinessofmedicine.net

www.ingramcontent.com/pod-product-compliance
Lightning Source LLC
Chambersburg PA
CBHW021501180326
41458CB00050B/6861/J